Praise for *Hal*

"After reading his prior books, the new book offers priceless insights and is an easy read. Hal discusses tactical sales techniques, but there are also philosophies that can increase personal motivation of any reader, no matter what thing or idea we're selling."

—Mick Fleming, president,
American Chamber of Commerce Executives

"Hal Becker never fails to deliver keen insights into how salespeople can succeed. This book is a useful tool whether you are new to sales or a seasoned professional!"

—Jon Diamond, CEO, SafeAuto

"Hal has given us a fabulous new book and veritable training guide to help anyone increase sales, regardless of whether you are selling a product or service. You will enjoy the quick and breezy style of his approach to sales."

—George Bernstein, CEO, Nobel Learning Communities
and former president of Pearle Vision

"Hal has another winner here. His insight and sales knowledge has helped our firm rededicate ourselves to selling with respect to professional services."

—Gary Shamis CPA,
SS&G Certified Public Accountants and Advisors

"Hal Becker understands that common sense, hard work, and incorporating the art and science of sales are essential for success as a sales professional. This book provides those tools for the salesperson to achieve those results."

—Bill Sublette, chief sales officer, TruGreen

"Hal engages sales reps with his wit, street smarts, and no-nonsense style. *Hal Becker's Ultimate Sales Book* is a fast-paced and easy-to-read sales classic, jam-packed with review and follow-up materials that guarantee you get results."

—Bob Silvy, VP corporate marketing,
American City Business Journals

"Hal's latest book is filled with stories, serious selling methods, and ideas that you can implement after reading each chapter. After working with Hal for a number of years and reading his latest book, *Hal Becker's Ultimate Sales Book*, all I can say is that "he walks the talk" and is our go-to sales trainer for obvious reasons. I know that you will love this book. I did!"

—John Brennan VP strategic relationship management,
The Hartford

"Hal is a master at taking complicated sales concepts and explaining them in ways that can be easily understood, even by those who are not career sales professionals. His techniques are proven and extremely helpful for business executives and owners who have ultimate responsibility for the sales success of their organizations."

—Rick Chiricosta, CEO, Medical Mutual of Ohio

"Just when you thought there could never be another meaningful sales book published, Hal brings us another winner. His typical wit and common sense approach puts his 30-plus years of experience between the covers of this sales manual and makes it relevant for today. What a great book!"

—Jerry Cox, president, Total Training Network

"Becoming an exceptional sales professional is not easy, but once again Hal has laid out the path to achievement with remarkable clarity, confidence, and practical application. A must-use for every organization seeking to improve its sales performance."

—Mark Kramer, CEO, Laird Plastics

"Hal shares his valuable real world sales insights in a straightforward, no-nonsense book. The information he provides will benefit any salesperson regardless of his or her experience."

—Ara Bagdasarian, EVP, Travel Centers of America

"As a proven number-one sales professional, Hal has a way of incorporating his vast knowledge of sales, business sense, and human nature into making him a top sales trainer and author that people actually listen to. *Hal Becker's Ultimate Sales Book* will give you valuable insights and spearhead your sales skills to the next level."

—David Scott, president and CEO, FM Turner

"Hal, once again, effectively breaks down the complexities of the sales process and shows us how to very simply execute to the desired result."

—Jerry L. Kelsheimer, president and CEO
Fifth Third Bank, Northeastern Ohio

Hal Becker's
Ultimate Sales Book

Hal Becker's Ultimate Sales Book

A Revolutionary Training Manual
Guaranteed to Improve Your Skills and
Inflate Your Net Worth

By Hal Becker

With Nancy Traum

CAREER
PRESS

Pompton Plains, NJ

HAL BECKER'S ULTIMATE SALES BOOK
Cover design by Rob Johnson
Printed in the U.S.A.

To order this title, please call toll-free 1-800-CAREER-1 (NJ and Canada: 201-848-0310) to order using VISA or MasterCard, or for further information on books from Career Press.

The Career Press, Inc.
220 West Parkway, Unit 12
Pompton Plains, NJ 07444
www.careerpress.com

Library of Congress Cataloging-in-Publication Data
Becker, Hal B.
    Hal Becker's ultimate sales book : a revolutionary training manual guaranteed to improve your skills and inflate your net worth / by Hal Becker, with Nancy Traum.
        p. cm.
    Includes index.
    ISBN 978-1-60163-241-8 -- ISBN 978-1-60163-557-0 (ebook)
        1. Selling. 2. Sales personnel. I. Traum, Nancy. II. Title.
HF5438.25.B423 2012
658.85--dc23
                                                        2012019953

To my late father and late mother, Joseph and Eunice, who taught me everything, including the principles by which I have always lived. My only regret is that they are not here to share this moment that is the culmination of everything they gave me.

To my wonderful wife, Holly, whose sense of humor, kindness, and true love make each day better than the last. To my daughter, Nicole, who has reminded me to play more, laugh, not stay mad for more than five minutes, and to keep that child inside of me, always!

Thank you.

Acknowledgments

To Nancy Traum, my editor, who makes my 5th grade writing look more mature—almost like an adult's!

To all my teachers who gave me a C or lower in English (just remember anyone can be an author).

To all my friends (you know who you are), who really are like my family and who have made my life more enjoyable with their incredible loyalty, love, and willingness to get off the couch and do stuff.

To my bandmates, be it the DooWops, Flashback, or Backtraxx, for allowing me to play drums with you and have so much fun entertaining audiences wherever we go.

To Don Riemer, who really has done nothing for this book, but maybe by mentioning him here, he will give me a couple of his very expensive sport jackets. We wear the same size!

To my wonderful clients, who during the last three decades have allowed me to help their business and/or train their staff.

To my very patient agent, Jeff Herman, who has a more warped sense of humor than I do.

To the doctors and researchers at the University of Indiana and to those who created the chemotherapy that saved my life and allowed me to enjoy my passion of writing books.

To the doctors and staff at University Hospitals in Cleveland, for utilizing an experimental program and treating me with compassion and incredible focus, giving me the second chance to really enjoy life.

To the staff at Career Press, who worked so hard on this project with me and have the dedication to create a great partnership.

To Joe Regano, superintendent of the Solon Schools; Tammy Strom, director of communications; Bill Nyerges, Solon High School art teacher; and the incredible students who did the fabulous illustrations: Priyanka Pai, Julie Selby, Kelsey McRill, Kathleen Zhang, Bobbie MacDougall, Margaret Li, and Amelia Sasak.

To everyone who will buy this book and try to become a better, more professional salesperson by actually *working on their profession* instead of just going through the motions.

Lastly, to everyone who gave me your knowledge, wisdom, and laughter, and made me a better person by just having a conversation with me.

Contents

Cold Calls, Phone Selling, and Other Contact Options

Time Management

Handling Objections

Setting Goals

Closing the Sale

Customer Care

Introduction

We all know there are many books out there that have been written on the subject of sales and how to sell. The question is, How many of those books actually *helped* someone to become a better salesperson?

This book is a different concept. It's a sales book and a sales training course rolled into one. You can read a little bit at a time or the entire book. Whatever your approach, the key is to retain the new information you learn and apply that information to your daily sales habits.

In this book, I combine the information from a number of articles I have written for syndicated publications. You will notice that many of them are quick reads that contain a lot of common sense and practical information that many salespeople have forgotten. I then set about incorporating my philosophy on selling, including the action steps that have worked so well for me. This combination has resulted in a practical, easy-to-read, one-of-a-kind collection that will improve your sales and hopefully make you enjoy the process more.

To get the most out of this book and your sales career:

- Stop at the end of every lesson and ask yourself, "How can I apply this to my situation?"

- Mark each important idea.

- Try reading each lesson twice before going to the next one.

- Remind yourself that you can and will succeed in sales, and every other endeavor, by building positive habits. Make a game out of building good habits. Reward yourself for every success.

- Use the ideas and principles in this book every day, in every situation.

- Review your progress at the end of every day. What did you do better? Where can you improve?

- Look for new ideas and examples around you.

What Makes a Good Salesperson?

"Remember, the secret to selling is sincerity. Once you can fake that, you've got it made."

Cartoon © Priyanka Pai. Used with permission.

My Cousin Arman's Lesson

Let me start by saying that I have a lot of really smart people in my family. I am not sure they all know this, but by comparison, I often feel pretty dumb.

One of my cousins is a cardiologist. Arman is not your typical, "let's just make the rounds" kind of doctor. He's much more. His bedside manner is outstanding, and he makes patients feel like they've known him all their lives. Arman has a soothing personality that makes patients feel he is looking out for them the way a friend would. Outside work, he's a regular guy whose favorite movies are *300* and *Star Trek*. He can talk about TV or movies all day long.

Arman is brilliant and his research exemplifies that point. He has written books and articles on just about every medical topic related to his specialty. He has a beautiful wife and adorable kids. He is the kind of guy that you sometimes want to hate, because you just can't measure up to his incredible talents and joy for life. We all love him, and he is wonderful to be around.

Now here's the part where I'm amazed. During one of our family dinners, he said something so profound that I sat back and was astounded by the powerful simplicity of his remark. We were talking about the aging of the population and how much money is spent on healthcare, especially in the final year or stages of someone's life. He said we spend 80 percent of our healthcare expenditures in our last year of life.

Arman added, "Isn't it amazing that (we) doctors do things *to patients and not for them*?" In other words, rather than always making the patient comfortable and doing what is best for the person, doctors sometimes choose the science or the procedure over the patient's quality of life. Wait, I know what you might say: it's all about saving the patient's life. We could have a long discussion on this subject, but in a second you'll see why I bring this up.

I started to think about this heavy, philosophical dilemma, and it hit me! Imagine if a professional salesperson could use the same concept while he or she sold to customers. It was so clear and simple. Most salespeople *sell to customers and not for them*. The typical salesperson is selling what is best for him and does not always have the best interests of the customer on his agenda.

Imagine if salespeople were taught to sell only what was best for the customer. Period! The salesperson would not have to think about his quota, commissions, or anything that concerned him other than the customer. He would focus on what was best for the customers, depending on their individual situations. Isn't this the kind of salesperson you would want to buy from, one who was always putting you first? Anyone reading this will be hard-pressed to remember dealing with a salesperson who sincerely put the customer first without compromise or hesitation. Have you ever had a salesperson tell you the outfit you selected was perfect, only to have friends or family tell you it looked terrible on you? Have you ever bought the latest, greatest gadget because the salesman's presentation was so powerful, only to come home and find that it either didn't work or you didn't really need it? The examples go on and on. When you do find a sincerely caring salesperson, don't you usually purchase more because you trust him?

Here is my challenge to anyone who wants to excel by being different. Think like my cousin Arman and put your patient—the customer—first. Then sit back and watch the way your sales grow, because customers trust you.

LESSON 2

Characteristics of a Top Salesperson

Studies show that most salespeople are either average or below average. Making your quota does not mean that you are successful. It means that you did enough to keep your job by producing at the expected level. Think about it. Would you want to go to a surgeon who said, "I performed the surgeries on the list, but didn't know a thing about the patient or why they needed the operation"? I don't know about you, but I want to be operated on by someone who is not only at the top of her profession, but also knows what is best for me and why.

I see many people in the training business or managers in a corporate sales environment who complicate something that's so simple. The question often asked is, "What traits do superior salespersons possess?" This question has been asked a thousand times and has been debated for decades. It has been addressed in hundreds of articles, studies, and books. It is so basic that many people don't believe the answer because it is too simple to be true.

The answer is discussed in one of the best articles I've ever read on sales, titled "What Makes a Good Salesperson," by David Mayer and Herbert M. Greenberg. It appeared in *The Harvard*

Business Review in August 2006, and was based on a previous article and study done in April 1961. The results of 50 years ago are the same today, because the premise is something that hasn't changed. According to the article, the two traits that make a successful salesperson are *empathy* and *ego drive.*

Empathy is the important ability to feel as the other person does. Most salespeople do not have empathy. They tend to put the customer second and not first. The salesperson usually thinks of just himself. Fabulous salespeople put the customer first and not the sale. One way to develop empathy in your sales work is by thinking about how you would you like to be treated.

Ego drive is the personal desire to make a sale. A successful person's ego drive will make her feel personally victorious when she makes a sale. When she fails, it pushes her to work harder, rather than find excuses or become discouraged.

The article states that there needs to be a balance between the salesperson's desire to empathetically help the customer and the need to succeed. If the balance is off, the result is a salesperson being liked for being "nice," but not necessarily making the sale or, conversely, a pushy salesperson who may force some sales, but miss many others because of his or her off-putting lack of empathy.

Of course, we need other skills in order to be a well-rounded salesperson. Product knowledge is vital, as is knowing how to handle objections, how to ask questions (as opposed to merely presenting), understanding the features and benefits of your products and services, and having good organizational skills. When these skills are developed and combined with empathy and a healthy ego drive, you have the makings of a successful salesperson.

Quiz 1

1. Above all else, a salesperson should focus on

   A. Increasing his commission.

   B. Quickly making a sale.

   C. Doing what's best for the customer.

   D. Distributing his business cards.

2. When you have empathy in sales, you tend to

   A. Put the customer first.

   B. Put yourself first.

   C. Watch sad movies.

   D. Hold therapy sessions.

3. Ego drive pushes a person to

   A. Not care about others.

   B. Make a sale.

   C. Make friends.

   D. Change careers.

What Great Salespeople Know

"Andy, when I tell you that you should know your competition, that doesn't mean inviting them to our office for a tour."

Cartoon © Julie Selby. Used with permission.

LESSON 3

Six Rules of Selling

When I first started my sales career at Xerox Corporation, I was taught a few things that have stayed with me for close to 35 years. These basic principles allowed me to be the number-one salesperson at Xerox out of a national sales force of 11,000, and have continued to bring me success in the businesses I have owned during the past two decades.

True salespeople follow six rules of selling that mirror the basic themes of every notable sales book. These principles have not changed in more than 75 years, and they probably will not change in the next 75. I learned the first three in 1976, at our Xerox training facility in Leesburg, Virginia, when I sat in a classroom for 12 to 14 hours a day, six days a week, for three weeks, getting an education in sales. The other three lessons I picked up in the last 20 years.

1. **Know your product.** We knew our copiers inside and out. We dreamt about them at night. We were responsible for retaining as much product knowledge as possible. We showed our customers that we knew our product and portrayed a strong sense of confidence. When you go shopping these days, how often do you

find salespeople who take pride in their products or spend time memorizing information about what they are selling?

2. **Know your competition.** You have strengths over your competitors, and you also have weaknesses. The same is true for your competitors. By learning what these are, you can compete with your competitors without knocking them. Don't give a customer the chance to say something nice about a competitor.

3. **Work harder.** Our quota at Xerox was simple: 10 new business contacts per day, whether it was a cold call in person or over the phone. I said to myself, "Hey, I can do more than that." So I set a new plan for myself: 20 calls per day. The key was that I made those calls every day! I ended up doubling everyone else's effort at more than 100 calls per week, 400 calls per month, 4,800 calls per year. The result was a simple, effective, and consistent plan that worked!

4. **Be organized.** Use your planner. Depend on it to the point that if you lost it, you would freak out. A planner can be a PDA, online scheduling program, or a paper day-planner. There are numerous products on the market to help you get organized. The important thing is to use whatever works best for you on a consistent basis. Use it to plan meetings with all prospects and your existing clients.

5. **Be assertive and consistent.** Assertiveness means being self-confident and self-assured, without being a pushy salesperson. It means never giving up and always being on top of the game plan. Focus, focus, focus. The more you do each day, the bigger the payoff. Remember that

the sales game is made up of customers you know and customers you haven't yet met.

6. **Be honest.** No sale is worth compromising your honesty. There is not a single sale you will ever make that will change your life. It might ensure a better month or even a better year, but it will not change your life.

   People buy from people, and in most cases, it's from people they like and trust. Those people are the ones we want telling others what a great job we did. If you have a reputation as an honest salesperson, your current customers will recommend you to others, which is an easy way to get referral sales.

Want a way to quickly remember the most important points? The sales warranty card on this page is basically an eight-hour sales class reduced to three simple concepts. These are the keys to success and will be for as long as you are in the sales profession.

Sales Warranty Card

This card is null and void if you fail to practice the following terms and conditions below:

To be the best, you are:

1. ORGANIZED—Use your daily planner and always keep in touch with clients and prospects.

2. ASSERTIVE—Small numbers multiply rapidly. Consistently make new sales calls EVERY day.

3. HONEST—All you have is your reputation. Let other people sell for you.

And remember:

- Selling is asking not telling, listening not talking.
- People buy from people.

Lesson 4

What Salespeople Can Learn From Kids

Good selling is based on probing. That means finding out what the customer wants or needs—not by talking, but by asking. Too many salespeople start by talking about themselves, often revealing way too much of their life history to make the customer feel they "know" them. They are now the customer's friend, because the customer knows where they went to school and that they are allergic to celery. They then talk about the company and its history. Finally, they go into detailed information about the product, how good it is, and what it will do for the purchaser. Add why the customer "needs" the product, and the salesperson feels they have done their job and done it expertly! Meanwhile, the customer tuned out at "celery" and is thinking about what they are going to have for lunch.

Rather than an endless presentation on the part of the salesperson, selling is a simple process of asking questions in a logical order to see if the customer's needs can be met. As you probe into the customer's situation even more by asking questions, their concerns will come to the surface, allowing you to address them.

Who can teach a salesperson about asking questions? Kids!

Typically, kids surpass adults at the number of questions they ask, because they are exceptionally curious. I admire how kids are able to excel in the area of communication. I've found that I can learn a lot by simply observing how kids interact with others.

You may have experienced this scenario: Your child wants a new toy, video game, or any kind of treat. He asks with no fear, even though he already thinks you are going to say no. In fact, he would be surprised if you were to say yes on his first attempt! The simple question is, "Mom, Dad, can I have the new, cool, battery-operated, handheld, electronic device that plays 568 games?" Unless he has straight As on his report card or you are trying to ~~bribe~~ reward him for good behavior, the answer is a simple "No." What does he do next? He goes into deep question mode. "How come? Why not? When can I? What if I...?" And that was only round one. Next round: "How come? Why not? When can I? What if I...?" The little tike will not quit until he either gets what he wants, or he is grounded until he is 40 years old.

Salespeople should imitate kids' natural fearlessness and curious approach when interacting with customers. Even before you get a no from a customer, be inquisitive and ask the customer about their views of their current situation and the product or service you are offering. Delve further by asking when or under what conditions they are likely to buy your product. By doing so, just like a kid, you're likely to uncover the reason your customer is hesitant and can work to create buying conditions that make both of you happy.

My advice is, before you make a sales call, either hang out with a kid or just take one along and watch them do their magic.

LESSON 5

Andy's Story

I'm usually pretty good at reading people. I say "pretty good" because that was until I met Andy. (I have changed his name to protect the innocent.)

In my line of work, I do two things: I give keynote addresses or speeches to large audiences on sales, customer service, or negotiating; and I do on-going sales training on a regular basis for a handful of companies. The latter is where I met Andy. His company asked me to work with their salespeople and address the lack of sales management. The first meeting is typically a meet-and-greet, during which I feel out the sales staff, and they do the same with me.

The man sitting next to me was a flashback from the 1970s. His suit was made of blue polyester with wide lapels, and he wore eyeglasses that even Elton John would not have worn in 1976. It was hard work ignoring the toupee he wore, because he had brown hair hanging out the back while the toupee was blonde. It reminded me of the time my mother wouldn't let me leave the house in fourth grade, because I wanted to wear a Beatles wig to school. My Beatles wig looked more natural than this guy's poorly crafted toupee.

The opinion I was forming in my head wasn't good. Was this the sales force I would be training? I was starting to feel like Sergeant Hulka in the movie *Stripes.*

The president of the company gave me some startling news when I asked, "Who in the room is your top salesperson?" He pointed to the gentleman sitting next to me with the toupee.

Okay, enough of being "Shallow Hal" and making fun of people. Here comes the best part. Because he was the best of the bunch, I started asking him a few questions. One of the responses he gave me was one that I will never forget!

He said, "My wife told me that the reason I am selling more and doing a better job is that I am focusing on the customer in front of me and not the sale." That was one of the most important things I have ever been told by a salesperson. It is so simple and yet so powerful. The message was clear.

Let's lay it out so everyone can understand this principal and use it every day while selling. If you truly understand and use this concept, you will be on the path to greatness in sales. This is sales success in a couple sentences: *Put customers first. Listen to them and their concerns, and forget talking about the product or service you're selling.*

That's it, the secret that we have been searching for all these years. It has always been there, but no one has really noticed how concise and simple it really is. Whether your suit is Armani or a couple decades old, if you are a genuine person and sincerely try to help the customer, your good intentions will come through, and you'll be successful in sales.

It's funny to me that when I see Andy from time to time, I don't notice the bad hairpiece; I notice what a good, caring person he is.

Quiz 2

1. Six things to know as a salesperson are

    A. Product, service, goals, pricing, sales script, great closes.

    B. Competition, getting up early, great presentation, features, handling objections.

    C. Getting there early, powerful voice, dressing well, good presentation skills, strong closes, utilizing daily planner.

    D. Know your product, know the competition, work harder, be organized, be aggressive, and be honest.

2. Honesty is important in sales, because all you have is your

    A. Friends and family.

    B. Money and lots of it from selling to suckers.

    C. Big home and really cool cars.

    D. Reputation.

3. A salesperson can learn from kids how to
   A. Skateboard.
   B. Write a sales proposal.
   C. Be fearless and ask probing questions.
   D. Be on time for appointments.

4. Andy was a top salesperson because he
   A. Dressed well.
   B. Had many friends.
   C. Was chummy with his manager.
   D. Focused on the customer instead of the sale.

The Importance of Listening

"Bob, you aren't listening to me: I don't want drapes covering my window when I've spent a fortune for a view of the city."

Lesson 6

Are You a Good Listener?

Listening is one of the most important aspects of any type of sale or negotiation, whether with professionals, friends, or family. Though most people think they are good listeners, the truth is quite the opposite: most of us need to improve our listening skills. Here is a simple exercise to test your listening skills. Reflect on your actions in the following situations:

- You just met several new people and were briefly introduced. Do you remember all of their names? Any of their names?

- You got lost and stopped for directions, which you didn't write down. Did you find your way? Or are you still lost?

- You are listening to someone and a thought pops into your mind. Do you interrupt the other person with your thought so you won't forget it? Or do you concentrate on your thought and wait until the other person is done without paying much attention to what he is saying?

- You are listening to someone who is speaking very slowly and it's driving you crazy. Do you interrupt and finish the sentence?

I'll bet you kept saying, "Yeah, I do that...and that...and that." Well, you just flunked. Welcome to the majority. The good news is that you can become a better listener. The bad news is that you have to practice for the rest of your life. To encourage you, let me say that once you succeed at becoming a better listener, others will enjoy being around you more because people love a good listener. This takes time and practice, and by the time you are 80 years old, you should have it mastered. The only problem is that you may have forgotten everything else!

Before we get to the tips on becoming a better listener in the next lesson, consider these ideas:

- It's easy to understand how emotions affect a sale or negotiation. We naturally prefer people who agree with us. Biased attitudes cause the listener to selectively hear the parts of your message that she is in agreement with or that reinforce her wants and needs. If the person you are speaking with forms an unfavorable opinion of you, and this judgment happens rapidly due to multiple factors, it's probable that she will not hear everything you say. The wall has gone up and, rather than listening, the person is actually busy forming objections to what you are saying.

- Think about the people you trust the most. Chances are they are close to you and know everything about you because they have listened to you through the years. Better yet, think of someone you know nothing about but will trust with your life, such as an airline pilot. You hope he or she is a good listener and can hear what is being said to him or her, so he or she can make accurate decisions. Without good listening skills, people in professions that deal with potential life and death situations can cause great harm. I always hope that my doctor, dentist, attorney, and airline pilot are diligent about working on their listening skills.

- It's possible to talk yourself out of a successful outcome or sale. I know people who have done this, but I have never heard of anyone who listened his or her way out of a successful outcome or sale. Remember that the most important part of negotiating or selling is to understand what the other party is really telling you.

LESSON 7

Become a Better Listener

Listening is a fascinating and complex skill, and like any other skill, it takes time and practice to develop. Remember to do the following when listening to another person:

- Encourage the other person to talk by being a good listener. That's the only way to learn what the other party wants.

- Limit your talking. You can't talk and listen at the same time.

- Ask questions if you don't understand something.

- Don't interrupt. Allow the other person time for pauses.

- Focus on what the other person is saying. Shut out distractions. If you're in a room that's very hot or cold, are you thinking about the temperature instead of what the person is saying?

- Take notes in order to remember important thoughts. You might not be able to remember everything the other party tells you. Note-taking makes a powerful impression because it shows you are not only listening, but that you want to remember what the person said after the meeting.

- Use interjections occasionally, such as "yes" or "I see," to show the person talking that you're listening and that you're with him or her. You can also use nonverbal interjections, such as occasionally nodding your head in agreement. Interjections encourage the speaker to keep talking. The best interviewers on television do this; it says, "I'm listening," and it keeps the person talking.

- Verify information when necessary. It's okay not to understand and to need clarification. You're conveying that you want to get the facts right.

- Paraphrase occasionally what the other person has said to be sure that what you hear is the meaning intended. Practice these examples (or similar phrases) until you can say them with conviction and enthusiasm: "What you're saying to me is..." and, "If I understand you correctly..." Good listeners paraphrase. It works! You get the clarification you need, and the other person senses that you are listening.

Your success as a salesperson can be directly influenced by your ability to listen more effectively. This is because the most important aspect of your job is to understand what customers are really telling you. Effective listening involves good comprehension and remembering as accurately as possible what has been said. It does not occur naturally; it's a skill that must be learned and practiced.

You normally think a great deal faster than you speak. This gap gives you "spare-thinking" time in conversations. One of the most important ways to listen more effectively is to learn to put this spare-thinking time to good use. A *Harvard Business Review* article, "Listening to People" by Ralph G. Nichols and Leonard A. Stevens (September–October 1957), offers four mental activities that will help you attend to all that is being said:

1. As you listen, try to predict the direction the speaker is taking and conclusions he will make. Be careful, however, not to pre-judge and stop listening.

2. Determine if the speaker is giving valid and/or complete support for the point he or she is making.

3. Occasionally summarize (to yourself) the points made so far. Summarize ideas and concepts, not facts.

4. Notice non-verbal cues. Search for meaning beyond the spoken words by paying attention to the speaker's body language, tone, and so on.

Be aware that emotions affect your listening ability. Your mood can affect how and what you hear. You tend to hear what you agree with, to the extent that objectivity can be lost and the validity of what is being discussed is obscured. If you hear something you strongly disagree with, you may sacrifice objectivity because you're preparing a rebuttal.

Lesson 8

The Power of Silence

Once, my wife and I went on a short cruise to Cabo San Lucas. We had a fabulous time, and I was finally able to prove something to her after multiple cruises. We, like most people, enjoy taking the shore excursions at each port, so we can have more experiences on our vacation.

I kept trying to convince my wife that at many ports, you can find the same shore excursions as those offered by the cruise ship, but for less than half the price. She didn't want to believe me. I said, "Just let me try it once, and if I'm wrong, the worst that can happen is we have one bad experience and then I get to say I'm sorry," which she loves to hear. When we got off the cruise ship, we saw at least 15 people holding signs that said "Whale Watching," the activity she wanted that day. I said, "Honey, why don't you pick which guy we should do business with?"

She picked Fernando, and I asked him, "How much for the whale watching tour?" He replied, "$80 for the two of you." This was less than the $90 they wanted per person on the ship. This was also when, though I was the customer in this case, I used a technique which I've learned during my years in sales: keeping silent.

I just stood there for maybe six or seven seconds and said, "Hmm," and he lowered his price to $70. I said to my wife, "What do you think?" She said, "Hmm." He then lowered his price to $60 for us both. Have you noticed that I haven't said a word to Fernando? He just kept lowering his price and basically negotiated with himself. I loved it!

Sometimes the best negotiating tactic you can use to get what you want is not to say anything at all. Just be silent and see what happens. It amazes me sometimes how easy things can be if you sit back and let things play out a little, and as they say, "watch the show."

As a salesperson, you can often let the customer do the talking, while you stay mostly silent. By doing so, you allow them to work out their own ideas, including what they need in a product or service, what terms would suit them, or how much they are willing to pay.

The next day, because we were at the same port for two days, I went back to Fernando to inquire about riding ATVs on the beach and desert. Again, I saved a bundle. I kept my mouth shut and said, "hmm" a few times. It was a blast. It's really hard not to have an ear-to-ear grin while you are tooling around in an ATV next to the ocean.

I think, on our next cruise, my wife will let me pick a couple more shore excursions. Unfortunately, I will still probably have to say, "I'm sorry" to her by the end of the week for something else that I messed up. But, it won't be because I didn't listen. Our vacations got better, because we both listened to what people were saying *before* we spoke.

Quiz 3

1. Listening is important to be a great

    A. Salesperson.

    B. Negotiator.

    C. Communicator.

    D. All the above.

2. Salespeople can talk themselves out of a sale, but can't

    A. Close the deal.

    B. Listen themselves out of a sale.

    C. Talk really fast so they can leave.

    D. Chew gum and walk at the same time.

3. An example of paraphrasing is

    A. "What you are saying to me is...."

    B. "Huh?"

    C. "What?"

    D. "Yeah, I couldn't agree more...."

Preparing for the Sales Call

"When I said you should prepare for your sales call, I meant put together a PowerPoint presentation."

Cartoon © Kelsey McRill. Used with permission.

Why Salespeople Fail

Most salespeople fail. It may seem hard to believe, but the majority of salespeople today don't make the grade. Walter A. Friedman, in the 2004 article "Birth of the American Salesman" published by Harvard Business School's *Working Knowledge*, states that in the year 2000, roughly 16 million salespeople were selling in the United States, and studies show that most salespeople are average or below average. That means only very few performed above expectations. When someone says to me, "Hey, Hal, I made quota this month," what that really means is that he or she just moved up from below average to average. That's like a baseball player saying, "Hey, Hal, I hit 150 last month." That doesn't impress me.

There are four simple reasons for failure, and they can be easily corrected once the problem is identified.

1. **You aren't enjoying what you do.** How can people be motivated if they hate their jobs or don't believe in their products or services? Sincerity and enthusiasm have to be genuine to be accepted—unless you are a fantastic actor, and then you should go into show

business instead of sales. If you don't like what you're doing, then quit and look for something that excites you. Imagine going to a restaurant where the chef didn't like to cook. I would imagine that the meal you were served wouldn't be too good, no matter how wonderful the service and atmosphere. Being good requires passion, or you're just going through the motions.

2. **You're not finding the right decision-maker.** It's easy selling to people who don't buy. They have no investment in learning from you and are just listening to pass the time or be polite. Though salespeople are hesitant to find the right decision-maker, because they are hard to reach and can give a firm no, they need to start from the top down. Always aim to speak to the person who has authority to approve a purchase, not someone who has to ask someone else to say yes. I would rather have a no from someone who can make a decision than stretching something out with no chance of a sale. Don't prolong a sale by talking to someone who has no decision-making capabilities. Just find out who can make the decision and then see what happens.

3. **Failure to ask questions and be curious.** Many salespeople like to talk just to hear the sounds of their voices. The best salespeople like to hear a little bit of silence. A good rule of thumb is that if you are doing more than 30 percent of the talking, you are telling and not selling. The customer should be doing most of the talking if you are asking the right questions. That's the reason you are there, to find out whether

you can help the customer, not just sell him something. The old saying, "He's such a good salesperson, he could sell snow to an Eskimo," is dead wrong. Eskimos don't need snow. They need a generator for assisting them with their electric needs if they are out in the wilderness. Be curious, and see whether you can help a customer, not just sell something.

4. **You're not making enough calls.** Make more calls to your current and potential customers. The number of calls made each day or month is a reflection of how much business a salesperson will produce. The more calls a salesperson makes to both groups, the more business a company will have, which of course turns into profitability for both the salesperson and his or her company.

What to Do Before the Sales Call

There is a big hole in training salespeople. This problem isn't new; it's been around for decades. The blame goes to the sales manager, entrepreneur, or person who is responsible for the salesperson. A typical salesperson is trained to start selling from the moment he walks in the customer's or prospect's door until the sale is made, or at least until he finds out why the person didn't buy. A *great* salesperson is trained to sell *before* he walks into the customer's building or office.

This is where the hole in sales training exists. If the salesperson understands the importance of *preparation* before the sales call, he or she will become much more successful. The points are fairly basic and have quite a bit of common sense attached to them. You won't find anything new or earth-shattering here, just several things we tend to forget along the way.

I can't express enough the importance of being prepared in selling or negotiating. As with any other event in life, preparation is essential. All professionals are prepared. The more prepared you are, the better your chance for success. For example, take a look at these professionals and their preparations:

- **Teacher:** A lesson plan is ready before every class. Imagine a teacher coming into the class with no preparation and saying, "Hey, kids, what do you want to do today?" A teacher must be prepared before walking into the classroom and must know exactly what he or she wants to accomplish. The teacher organizes and plans lessons in order to accomplish goals.

- **Lawyer:** Before every trial, a lawyer prepares notes on what he or she will cover in the courtroom. Don't you want your lawyer to have the questions written down and to have an idea of what he or she will ask witnesses before they take the stand? As one of the greatest trial attorneys of all time, Irving Younger, once said, "Never ask a question to which you do not already know the answer." The better prepared the lawyer is before the case, the better the client's chances of winning.

- **Dentist:** When your dentist walks into the room with your chart, he has your mouth's history in his hands. Do you think for a moment that you are the dentist's only patient? Does he sit around all day for six months, waiting for you to return? "Hurrah! Hal is here. Get me the drill!" He needs to look at your chart to remember what he did on your last visit and to check on what has happened in your mouth since then.

- **Physician:** Before an annual physical, your doctor has a sheet with your medical history. You want your doctor to ask you questions to determine what has changed and/or what new problems you may be experiencing. You don't want your doctor to walk in and greet you with, "Hey, let's do an appendectomy. No specific reason...just for the heck of it!" The better a doctor's notes from all your previous visits, the better the doctor's chances of taking into consideration your medical history and prescribing the proper treatment.

- **Professional golfer:** Golfers play the course a number of times before a match to become familiar with the course. You don't see a professional golfer showing up the day of the tournament and saying, "Hi, there! I'm ready to play! Does anybody know where the first hole is?" The more familiar a golfer is with the course, the greater his chances of winning. This familiarity also provides a great deal more confidence which results in a competitive edge.

- **Race car driver:** A race car driver goes through the course a number of times to get a feel for the track and to build confidence. In most races, the cars are fairly identical in construction, so the edge comes from the driver's skills, knowledge of the track, desire to win, and readiness to take risks to outmaneuver the other drivers.

- **Military special forces:** From the Navy Seals to the Army Rangers, these elite forces practice certain combat situations over and over again until they become procedures with which they are fully familiar. This practice gives them a higher degree of confidence before they enter a live military situation. The military refers to this approach to preparation as military muscle. It's said that any task or exercise that is repeated 2000 times becomes habit and automatic. The bottom line is that the special forces practice more and train harder than other branches of the military.

After all these years, I'm surprised there are so many people going on a sales call or walking into a meeting ready to negotiate that have failed to do advance preparation. Bottom line: The more you prepare before the meeting, the better chance you have to succeed. Before each meeting, you should:

- **Review your goals.** This is a fundamental step. I have asked hundreds of salespeople the following question when I am traveling, as we are about to exit the car to make the sales call: "Before you go into the customer's office, what is your goal?" The answer is usually, "I want to make the sale." I ask the next important question for a simple reason. "Is this the first time you are meeting the customer, or is this a sales call to close the customer?" The goal on the sales call can range from simple information-gathering to rapport-building or presenting a proposal. There are many types of sales calls, and subsequently many types of goals for individual sales calls.

- **Have your notes ready.** Have the questions you want to ask the customer in front of you on a piece of paper. Don't go in "winging it" or taking shortcuts. Go over the questions in the car before you make the sales call to see if everything you want to discuss is written down. This strategy is imperative and not open for discussion!

- **Avoid watching TV.** When you are in the lobby waiting to see your contact person in the company, don't watch TV if there is one in the lobby. That also applies to reading magazines. This is the time to notice things. Does the lobby have decor from 1960 or do they spend money to communicate a certain appearance? Look to see what plaques are on the wall and what message they are sending. The receptionist can be a wealth of information, and might be willing to engage in conversation with you and give you some pointers or inside information.

- **Leave your phone/Blackberry/iPhone in the car.** In today's high-tech world, we need to focus on the customer and not allow interruptions. Leave your cell phone, Blackberry, or iPhone in the car. That way, if a call or message comes in, you aren't distracted while you are in the customer's office. The precious little time we have in front of decision-makers should be embraced with enthusiasm and sincere attention.

- **Notice the customer's office and be real.** Little things tell us a lot. Look around the person's office and look at the pictures. Are they family photos or pictures of a car or boat? Is the person you are talking to in any of the photos? Notice things, try to connect the dots, and ask a question if something seems of sincere interest to you. People love to talk about themselves, provided the person asking the question is genuinely interested. It's easy to spot a phony or someone who is trying to make small talk for no particular reason. Be genuine, the kind of person you would like to have in your home.

The Proposal

I don't ever recall going to a sales training seminar or class that taught you how to write a proposal using simple, common sense. I'm sure there are courses out there somewhere that cover this subject. I'm not speaking about the grammar, punctuation, or even sentence structure of proposal writing. I'm referring to the kind of proposal you and I would like to read, and definitely something your client or customer would want to read as well.

Typically, a company's marketing department will instruct the sales staff on what makes a good or decent proposal. Following the training session, the salespeople are in control of what goes into the proposal and what reaches the prospect or client. In smaller companies, you often find an owner who started out selling his product and then moved to teaching his new salespeople how to write proposals based on how he did them. Using a generic proposal form developed by someone else in which you simply fill in the blanks or change the name of the client won't work.

Proposals should always be put together with the customer in mind. Cookie-cutter proposals often include information that is unnecessary, because they are meant to cover all situations. The sales rep or manager often thinks that thicker proposals are more impressive—the more information they pack into the proposal, the better. They include the company's history, a factual time-line of the industry and how it began, their mission statements, complete product line (past and present), a description of every employee with his or her biography, features and benefits of their product or service, lots of graphs and charts because they look impressive in color, and finally their pricing for the product or service.

Who are you trying to impress? No one wants to read through all that material. Think about it: if you were going to buy a cel-lular phone or an insurance policy for your home, do you want a 28-page proposal? I don't know about you, but all I care about is:

- Will the pricing be competitive?
- Will the product or service do what is said it will do?
- Can I trust the salesperson and the company, and rely on her in the future?
- Is the service going to be as good as the salesperson claims?

That's it, end of story. Don't complicate something that can be easy for both you and the customer. Customers want you to tell the truth, to get to the point, and to keep your promises. It's about a fair price and not having problems with the product or service once the sale is completed. Big, fancy proposals take up time that could be spent concentrating on the key values of your product or service. That's all customers want. If you give them too much, they'll only be confused and unable to sort out what your real value is and how it will benefit them. A strong proposal relies on easy communication of the key value of the product, not on a lot of extra and unnecessary information designed to confuse or intimidate the customer.

Did you ever observe your customers as they go through your proposal? If you did, you would have noticed that they often go right to the last page of the proposal because that's where the numbers are. If this is the case, presenting a proposal as big as *War and Peace* not only wastes their time, but yours as well. In addition, if they are skipping to the end, chances are they are not hearing what you're saying, but concentrating on the bottom line or cost.

Keep it simple, and present a compact and relevant proposal tailored to the customer's needs. The quicker you get to the key points you want to communicate, the quicker they will be able to make a decision if your product or service fits their needs. If your product or service isn't what they need, you have time to move on to another prospect.

Features Versus Benefits

Many salespeople think they know the difference between features and benefits. When quizzed, they don't even come close to mastering something tangible and important to the customer. When selling, *forget about features and get right to benefits.*

First, let's look at what a feature is. A feature is what something is made up of, or a part of the product. An example of a feature on a new car is an eight-cylinder engine. Another feature is 12 air bags—front, back, and on all sides. Yet another feature might be a GPS in the dashboard or heated seats.

A benefit is what the feature does for the customer. The benefit of an eight-cylinder engine is that the car goes faster. The benefit of 12 air bags is that passengers have a greater chance of survival in case of an accident. The benefit of the GPS is that the driver will never be lost, and the heated seats will keep the rider toasty in cold weather.

Advertisers use features all the time in their commercials. Did you ever see the commercial for the breath mints called Certs? If you did, you probably remember their active ingredient called Retsyn. Did you ever see a Retsyn? If you did, would you recognize it on the street? Of course not, but the feature is Retsyn, and the benefit is that it keeps your mouth minty fresh.

For years, Chrysler advertised their cars by saying they had "cab-forward design." What the heck does that mean? Who cares! The benefit is what was important, and that was simple and straightforward—you had more leg room and head room. I hope that you are getting the idea now and that anytime you give a feature, you *must* follow it up with a benefit.

I usually don't like it when people take shortcuts, even though I took them frequently until my late 20s (please don't tell my daughter). I'm going to give you one now. It's okay to do this in any sales situation. Here's the shortcut: you don't have to give features.

Yes, I said it: you do not have to give features. In most cases, features are meaningless, and they really don't sell anything. What sells a product or service are the benefits. Remember that the benefit is what the customer is buying! She wants the benefit that appeals to her, not you. By focusing on her needs, you will sell more and not waste your time talking about things the customer didn't even care about in the first place.

Quiz 4

1. To be successful as a salesperson you must

    A. Talk to anyone you can.

    B. Get a yes from anyone in the company.

    C. Find the right decision-maker.

    D. Talk to all the decision-influencers.

2. When a salesperson goes on a sales call, she should be

    A. Ready to do battle as she enters the client's office.

    B. Have donuts with her at all times.

    C. Be prepared for the call.

    D. Have many free samples ready to hand out.

3. What should you not do when you are in the lobby before the sales call?

    A. Go over your goals.

    B. Look at your notes.

    C. Take notice of things around you.

    D. Watch TV.

4. When you are on the actual sales call

    A. Have your Blackberry/iPhone always on, in case a big client calls.

    B. Leave your phone in the car. Focus on the customer.

    C. Put your phone on their desk. It makes you look important.

    D. Tell your spouse to call at a certain time and pretend they are a VIP.

5. When putting together a proposal, always

    A. Keep it simple.

    B. Make it complicated.

    C. Use Arial font.

    D. Make it as least 50 pages.

6. A feature is

    A. What the product or service does.

    B. Meaningless without a good price.

    C. After the coming attractions.

    D. Everything to the customer.

7. A benefit is

    A. Health insurance and a pension.

    B. Meaningless without a good price.

    C. What the product or service costs.

    D. What the product or service does to help the company or individual.

The Importance of Questions

"Bill, I told you that a great salesperson should ask a lot of questions, but not about someone's religion or sexual preferences."

Cartoon © Kathleen Zhang. Used with permission.

LESSON **13**

Questions Are Everything in a Sale

In 1936, Dale Carnegie wrote his best-selling book, *How to Win Friends and Influence People.* In the book, he said the secret was to find out what people wanted. That couldn't be any truer today. It's so simple, yet so few salespeople do it.

Find out what people want. The only way to do that is to ask questions and listen to the answers. That means quit the sales-pitching presentations and all the spewing of wonderful product knowledge you have memorized.

I actually observed a salesperson who was so into his memorized presentation that when the customer interrupted to ask a question, his response was, "That's a good question. The answer to that will be covered later in the presentation." How absurd! Good salesmanship goes hand in hand with good customer service, and the salesperson missed a golden opportunity to give the customer what she needed in a timely fashion. By not answering the question, he was sending the message that his well-rehearsed presentation was more important than giving her the information she needed. It also set the standard for future interaction with the client, and such negative impressions are hard to reverse once created.

Selling is simple when you break it down to this core: don't tell—ask! The more questions you ask, the more you will find out what the customer is and isn't interested in. You will find out his past buying history and what he wants now and in the future. The key element of success for professional salespeople is the nature of questions they ask and what information they walk away with.

How many questions should you ask? As many questions as you think are necessary. If you are wondering what kind of questions you should ask, here are some ideas to get you started:

- What is the customer's decision-making level? Does he have the authority to buy?

- What has he bought in the past and why?

- Is he happy with his current vendor? Why or why not?

- Who was his previous vendor and why did he switch?

- What would he change about his current vendor and why?

- What is important to him and his company?

These are just a few examples of some basic yet important questions you should ask a customer. It doesn't matter in what order you ask them or even how you ask the questions. You just have to be sincere, show you care, and come across as an expert regarding your product or service. A good rule is to ask questions 70 percent of the time and talk no more than 30 percent during your interview or sales session with a customer.

This isn't something that will necessarily come easy to you in the beginning. It takes practice, and the more you practice, the better you will get. As time goes by, you will find yourself at ease with asking questions. Incidentally, this will eventually carry over into your personal life as well, and you will find yourself discovering more about people, whether they are your co-workers, friends, or family members.

People love to talk. The best way to get them to do that is to ask questions and then listen. Be concerned, curious, and empathetic. Sometimes it's best to tell the customer "no" if he or she doesn't really need your product or service. That would mean being very honest, another great attribute of a top salesperson, and something that will impress the heck out of the customer, and deepen the trust you have just established for future transactions.

Past, Present, and Future

I was having a discussion with a friend and was giving him some pointers on effective salesmanship. We were talking about the importance of questions during the sales call and why it's necessary to use them. My friend understood the concept, but the application wasn't truly sinking in.

During my explanation of the logic of the questioning process, something just came out of my mouth, and it even surprised me. I said, "You have to fix the past before you can move on to the present and future!" I thought to myself, "Hal, you have to remember this for future reference, because it's really good!"

As I've said before, your goal in any sales call is to learn about the customer, her company, and what she wants. The only way to extract this information is to ask questions and discover what she is thinking. Talking about yourself or your business will not accomplish your objective.

In so many sales calls, I've seen the customer not wanting to do business or even talk about the possibility of buying from the salesperson. The frustration is evident in the customer's tone, body language, or lack of participation in the sales call. At this point, even though you might still be in the customer's office, the sales call is basically over. You might as well get up, thank her for her time, get into your car, and then tell your boss that it was an unsuccessful appointment.

What can be done to avoid this scenario? Things will change forever if you start to practice the following advice. Every sales call should be set up as a fact-finding mission with you as the explorer. Before you discuss the present, you need to find out about the past. Did the customer have a bad experience in the past with a salesperson who sold your product or service? Did the product he purchased work as promised? The client's hesitation to discuss your product could have nothing to do with you and everything to do with a negative past experience from which he or she hasn't fully recovered.

Before bringing up a new subject, ask questions about the past. These could include questions about the relationship between your company and theirs. Who did they deal with? What products or services did they use in the past? Were there any complaints or problems? If this goes well, move to the present.

If there was a problem in the past, stay there and do whatever you can to repair the issue. Don't move on to the present until you've done everything you can to fix a past problem. A word of caution: Not every problem can be fixed. All you can do is try, and that effort alone is going to impress the customer regardless of the outcome.

The customer will appreciate that you are learning about him and his concerns. If the past is fine, the present looks good, and he is content with doing business with you, now you can move ahead to the future. No, you are not Marty in *Back to the Future* and there is no DeLorean. You are just ready to move forward with the sale! At this point, you can discuss a framework for the future of your two companies doing business together. This could be a long term contract, a beta test of a new product or service, or even a partnership.

Wherever you go at this point should work out well, because you have already uncovered what the customer liked and didn't like about past experiences with your company and fellow employees. You could even discover some policies or procedures that the customer thought needed improvement. Take these ideas back to your company and, provided they are good ideas, you will be the hero!

This concept will never fail you because you are uncovering the customer's history and past concerns, and not just talking about what you can do for them in the present.

Lesson 15

All You Need Is
One Question

I am the first to admit that I'm not good at networking. I don't like small talk and I'm very uncomfortable going into a room with people I don't know, walking up to a stranger, and starting a conversation. When I'm out of town to give a speech or conduct a seminar and I visit the cocktail reception the night before to acquaint myself with my clients, it's usually a very short visit. I often find myself doing a quick lap around the room looking for the cheese and vegetable appetizers, and then I'm off to my hotel room to order room service.

Now you understand that I'm not qualified to discuss networking or how to work a room, because I both can't and don't like to network. What I do want to do is build relationships, and that takes a lot more time than the obligatory two-hour meet-and-greet cocktail reception. Because it's hard to build a relationship with 100-plus people during one of my presentations, I prefer to concentrate on building a relationship with the client who hired me. The first step to doing that is to be prepared when I deliver the product (in this case, myself and my knowledge) by asking questions about the audience and what they want to learn. Knowing who the audience is also prepares me for answering any questions that may arise either during or following my presentation.

I remember reading a book about 20 years ago that gave some advice about what to do if you meet a famous person. It said not to fawn over her or say what she hears from everybody else, such as, "Oh, I just love your new movie. I think you're great." Instead, ask a question! Ask a question that is sincere and different from what she typically hears. Ask something you would want to answer if you were on the receiving end of the question. This requires that the person talk to you to answer your question. The conversation will be more genuine if you're not discussing something such as the weather or the local traffic conditions. Try to make the conversation fun, real, and different from what she usually encounters.

Let's say you met George Clooney, an actor with a great sense of humor who loves practical jokes. Ask him, "What was the best practical joke you've ever played on someone?" Chances are, he will answer you because the question is different and something that he enjoys talking about.

So, let's assume you're at a big company meeting and you notice your company's CEO and want to introduce yourself. Go over and say, "Hello, my name is Hal, and I work in the sales department. I'd like to ask you one question. What is the one accomplishment you're most proud of since you've been with our company?" I guarantee the CEO will want to give you the answer and will be impressed that you even asked! Why? Because this question is about him and not you!

This scenario can be used in other circumstances besides networking. When I was in Las Vegas, a person I was introduced to at dinner was discussing the problems he was having at the hotel.

Apparently, housekeeping had overlooked his room and it hadn't been cleaned in three days.

Assertive person that I am, I said, "Let's go to the front desk, ask for the manager, and get you compensated for this lack of customer service."

We headed to the front desk to speak to the manager. Rather than get right to the complaining, I decided to practice what I preach and asked her, "What was the worst problem or incident you ever had to take care of?" She laughed a little and said, "Oh, sir, there really has never been one." I asked again, this time saying, "Oh, come on, there has to be one." I didn't get her to give me a juicy story, but my new dinner friend got a free night's stay and lots of drinking credits for the bar!

In most situations, including networking and selling, a well-thought-out question can serve as an instant connection to people you just met. It not only piques their interest in you, but it entices them to share interesting information about themselves, creating a channel of communication between you.

Lesson 16

Part A and B Selling

There are millions of salespeople who have never been properly trained. There are lots of courses available, and the ones who know what they're teaching are all saying pretty much the same thing: the role of the salesperson is to find out what the customer needs or wants, and then to provide that service or product if possible.

I don't know who developed this type of sales training or if there is even a name for it. For sake of simplicity, let's just call it Part A and B selling. I've seen this on many sales calls, more than I would have ever wanted to witness firsthand, and I know I will continue to see it in the future. Part A is when the salesperson asks the obligatory questions, and Part B is when the salesperson tells everything about himself, his company, and what his product or service does.

Maybe it's a natural reaction that causes this type of behavior on a sales call. I know firsthand that other sales trainers or consultants, including me, would never train this method of selling in which you ask a few questions and then simply dump information. Great selling is genuine dialog in action. Find out all you can about the customer rather than "verbally vomiting" all over him with your information.

What is troubling is that many salespeople practice Part A and B selling so much that they are perfecting something that is **basically wrong and poor selling**. For example, the salesperson will come to the sales call prepared with his questions and proceeds to do what he is supposed to do. He asks a series of questions, and hopefully listens to the customer to find out what is on the customer's mind. So far he is right on track.

At this point, things change. The salesperson assumes he has all the information he needs and he switches to talking mode. He has completely flip-flopped the sales process and is now in what he thinks is Part B: providing information on the product or service. However, what he is now doing is talking 100 percent of the time about his company, its history, mission statement, how many locations it has, and the employee roster. There is such a thing as too much information, and most customers don't want or need this overkill of facts. The only way to find things out is to ask them—not tell them.

When the salesperson talks too much, the customer is likely to get bored. In my role as a sales call observer, I pay attention to the customer's facial expressions and body language. The customer is too often simply being polite and pretending to listen rather than actually hearing what the salesperson is saying. More likely, he is thinking about what he is going to have for lunch or whether he will make his 5 p.m. tee time at the golf course. The salesperson feels it is necessary to get all his information out at this juncture of the sales call. Wrong!

Bottom line, the salesperson should be asking questions throughout the sales call and providing the answers that specifically address the questions asked. That way he can have a normal dialogue that is a two-way communication, and both parties can participate by asking questions, listening, and having a more balanced conversation.

Forget Part A and B selling, and just make it Part A.

Lesson 17

The Magic Question

The magic question is a must for any person in sales. It's probably the most important tool in the salesperson's bag. The problem is that not many people know about it.

To understand the idea behind the magic question, one must go back to the basics and understand the concept of selling. You've heard this before: selling is asking, not telling; it's listening, not talking. If you have been trained to just present your product or service, scrap everything you've learned. Take the training books you've been using and anonymously donate them to your competitor's company. Then start over.

What is the magic question? I'm going to answer that question with another question. "Will you tell me about the ongoing sales training that you participate in at your company?" As a sales trainer, that's *my* magic question.

The response I receive when asking my magic question is likely to be that they don't have any ongoing sales training. Now I've got them. It's my conversation from this point on. I could respond that they must have something, or if their comment is true, I ask why don't they have ongoing sales training. Now the conversation will go in the way I would like to take it, because it's my job to prove why they need sales training.

I'm pretty much done if they answered that the company does use an ongoing sales training program. At that point, I might remind myself how important it is to remember that the best salespeople can't sell everybody. If you are really good, you know when to advise the company to continue doing what it has been doing and walk out.

Your magic question should be one to get the customer to open up and want to talk about the area you are trying to discover. It has to be sincere and right to the point. Though your own magic question should take time to develop and should be modified for each selling situation, here are some examples. If you are selling cars, you could say, "What are your driving habits like?" If you are selling an intangible (a service rather than a product) such as health insurance, you could say "Can you provide me details about the health coverage you have for your employees?" You could even use it if you are a CPA; ask a potential client, "Do you feel that you might be paying more taxes than you should?" Don't try to be trite or cute. It has to be a real question that the customer has not heard from every other salesperson.

Here are some important points to consider when formulating your magic question:

- Take your time and think about what you want to ask. My magic question took me 14 years to formulate.

- Know when to use the magic question. It isn't a closer; it's a way to get the customer to talk about the subject matter you want to discuss. It's a door opener, and the more honest and sincere you are, the more likely you'll get an answer.

- Try to put the magic question into as few words as possible. "Less is more" is especially true with the magic question. The more the customer talks, the more you will learn.

- Once you use your magic question, you'll find the game of sales is a lot more enjoyable and that you have more control of the conversation.

LESSON 18

The Questionnaire

As I've said before, the formula is simple: ask questions rather than talking and boring the customer to death about how great you and your company are. This way, you are finding out what the customer wants rather than telling her what you want to sell. The real pros always have the questions to ask in front of them, so they stay on track and know what to ask through the course of the sales meeting.

The following Simple Sales Questionnaire is conceptual in nature. It's a template that you can copy, play around with, add to, delete from, or change to fit your style and personality.

SIMPLE SALES QUESTIONNAIRE

Client Name:

Customer Profile Date:

Company:

Phone:

Fax:

E-mail:

Address:

Contact/Title:

Operations

How long have you been with the company?

How many employees?

Other locations?

Decision-Making

Who beside yourself participates in the decision making process?

Usage

How much?

Quantity:

Stock:

Amount/Misc.:

Methods

Current vendors / previous vendors:

How long? Why?

Dissatisfaction (Most important!)

What would you change about your current vendor if you could change anything?

Consequences (Refer to answer of dissatisfaction.)

How does this affect you?

Value (Refer to answer of consequences.)

What would it mean if I could provide [the benefits of your product or service]?

Now you can talk about:

1. Higher quality

2. Easier operations

3. Lower cost

Trial close: "If we could provide you the best product/service at a competitive price and improve your present situation, would you consider working with our company?"

◆◆◆

Let's go through each area of the questionnaire. Let's assume that this is a first visit and that you want to engage the prospect to build trust.

- **Operations:** This section lets the customer know that you're interested in his or her business. This allows the prospect to talk about the company. If possible, get a tour during this section to provide you with an insider's view of the company.

- **Decision-Making:** You need to know who you should be talking to and who can actually make the decision.

- **Usage:** Allows you to concentrate on the portion of the business that will use the products or services you can provide.

- **Methods:** This gets you information about your competitor or who the prospect is currently using to provide the product or service. This is a crucial point: *never knock the competition.* By doing so, it tells the customer or prospect that he or she made a mistake or was stupid to do business with the competition.

- **Dissatisfaction:** Using questions, find the prospect's level of satisfaction or frustration with the current vendor. If you were completely satisfied with something, would you change? I know that I wouldn't! This area tells you whether to move forward or to call it a day and find a new prospect. Some salespeople might consider it a challenge to take a happy customer away from a competitor. This is more about their egos than good selling. Someday the company's current salesperson may move or retire, and you want to leave every prospect with a positive impression of you in case you have the opportunity to present to him or her again in the future.

- **Consequences:** This allows you to get the customer to talk about the problems, so he or she can revisit the negatives about the current vendor. Just sit back, listen, and enjoy the show!

- **Value:** Here all you have to do is listen to the customer's area of dissatisfaction and restate it in question form. Example: "What would it mean to you if I could provide [the benefits of your product or service]?"

It's time to put what you just learned into action. What questions can you develop to improve your ability to qualify a prospect in each of the following areas?

- Operations and decision-making
- Usage

- Methods
- Dissatisfaction
- Consequences and value

[ACTION STEP]

What questions can you develop to improve your ability to qualify a prospect in each of the following areas?

A. Operations and decision-makers

1.

2.

3.

B. Usage

1.

2.

3.

C. Methods

1.

2.

3.

D. Dissatisfaction

1.

2.

3.

E. Consequences and value

1.

2.

3.

What is your magic question?

Quiz 5

1. In the course of the sale, it is best to
   A. Ask questions.
   B. Talk about your company.
   C. Explain features and benefits.
   D. Give an award winning presentation.

2. How many questions should you ask a customer or prospect?
   A. 10.
   B. 100.
   C. As many as you think are necessary.
   D. As few as possible.

3. Asking questions in the sales process

   A. Should come naturally to you.

   B. Should be very uncomfortable.

   C. Should not be looked at as important.

   D. Will take practice, like anything else you do.

4. Your goal in any sales call is to

   A. Learn as much about the customer as you can.

   B. Close the deal as fast as you can.

   C. Sell as much as possible even if the customer doesn't need it.

   D. Not leave without an order.

5. When on a sales call

   A. Talk about your agenda, and focus only on what you want to say.

   B. Avoid the past, because it may be a problem.

   C. Look for ways to sell to the customer as quickly as possible.

   D. Ask questions about the past.

6. If there is a problem with the past

   A. Ignore it.

   B. Repair it.

   C. Just say "I'm sorry."

   D. Find the nearest exit and leave.

7. Your magic question should

   A. Perform miracles.

   B. Hypnotize your customer.

   C. Get the customer to talk about the area you want to explore.

   D. Entertain children.

Increasing Your Sales

"Tom, though you won't buy from me, can I have a bunch of referrals?"

Cartoon © Bobbie MacDougall. Used with permission.

How to Increase Sales

Great salespeople understand the balance of keeping their existing clients while always looking to attract new business. As time goes by, clients' habits change. They might go in a different direction or even change vendors with no apparent motive. For that reason, a salesperson must try to explore new ways to build his prospect base and eventually add new clients or customers.

There are ways to keep or add new customers by using a combination of selling and marketing. A great company with strong marketing tools can make this task easier with a good database and a well-thought-out method of how to attract business that suits their industry. For some, it might be as simple as a cold call or a telemarketing team to make numerous phone calls. For others, such as a lawyer or an accountant, it might be joining a country club or getting on boards to create new relationships. Some businesses need to do as many trade shows as they can each year for exposure to their marketplace. There are numerous ways to add new customers, and each company has to figure out what's best for them and their sales staff.

Today, companies are turning to social media to help them sell their product or service. The increase in companies with a social media presence (on Facebook, YouTube, Twitter, LinkedIn, and so on) has been phenomenal and will continue to grow as business turns to new ways to sell and market their product. I'm not a Twitter kind of guy, nor do I believe people follow my sales training on FaceBook. What I do know is that these areas of marketing and promotion can't be ignored by a company with a sound and future-driven marketing plan. Here are some things to consider when using social media:

- Do the various applications fit the demographics of your audience?

- Do you and your company have access to the technology to support social media?

- Have you made the commitment to keep your information current and relevant?

- Do you have the time to devote to social media without abandoning other aspects of your sales plan?

The following is a breakdown of different methods to increase sales:

- For existing customers:
    - Stay in touch often.
    - Ask how satisfied/dissatisfied they are.
    - Get customers to want to refer you.
- For new business:
    - Learn how to get past the screen (to be discussed in Lesson 22).

- ➤ Use phone, a cold call, or e-mail to get an appointment.

- ➤ Consistently make attempts to find new customers each day.

- For networking:

  - ➤ Join your local chamber of commerce, Rotary, and so on.

  - ➤ Be visible in your community.

  - ➤ Make people want to do business with you by volunteering.

True Relationships Are Built Slowly

I find many salespeople think the key to selling is networking and constantly searching for new business in addition to the business they already have. I have no problem with that concept if it works for them in a high percentage of cases. This method is not restricted to one certain business or industry. Networking may be an effective way for some to increase business, if the salesperson stays focused and is consistent in his or her approach.

Nevertheless, I don't always agree with the concept of networking, and I don't teach it in my seminars. I have always believed in being more focused on spending quality time with people who make a difference in my life and my career. In other words, I focus on building relationships, which is actually the purest form of networking.

Real networking is about building relationships, not selling. The relationship building I have done in my life has been to make acquaintances and to be visible in my community and industry. Have you ever been to a function where people are "networking" and the salespeople in the group are seeing how many business cards they can distribute? Based on a 60-second encounter, how many of the people they met do you think will call them the next day and ask to purchase their product or service? They will probably remember the salesperson as slightly obnoxious, because all he cared about was the number of people he could hand his card to—no one likes to be a statistic. The salesperson usually asks for the prospect's business card and then follows up with a phone call the next day: "Remember me? We met for 60 seconds yesterday at the XYZ function, and I gave you my business card." Now the prospect is even more annoyed, because he or she realizes that the salesperson is only interested in one thing: selling his product. People do business with people they know, like, and trust, not someone they met for 60 seconds at a function.

Let's discuss what would be a more fine-tuned method for creating great relationships in the business community:

- **Work on existing relationships.** Look at your clients or customers and decide where you can be an asset to them, and what you can learn from them. Business is not always about what you can get from someone else. In a good working relationship, both parties are learning and developing a deeper understanding of each other. The better the relationship between you and the other party, the more business you will acquire. If you are good at your profession, others will refer you to their friends and associates, leading to more business. The key is to be sincere and to not make generating more business as the sole basis of your relationship. The other party will sense if you are only interested in generating referrals, and this can work against you. When you are empathetic and show genuine concern for your client, the rest will follow and more business will be a result of the relationship, not the cause.

- **Pick the relationships you want.** We all have busy lives, and time seems to go by faster as we age. Ask people over 50, and they will verify this fact. The people you surround yourself with in your personal and business life reflects who you become.

  Decide who you want to spend your time with and why. Carefully pick a number of clients or customers with whom you can go to the next level in your relationship. When you think through the process, look at your relationships as a game plan. You will find yourself more organized in your thinking and in your business career.

- **Decide what new business you want.** Be proactive, seeking out specific customers, rather than reactive, taking whoever comes along. Decide which customers you'd like to have and why. For instance, if I wanted a new client, regardless of location, I would first evaluate the potential for income.

  Next, I would look at the logistics, or where I will spend my time. If the client or customer is headquartered in San Diego and I am in Cleveland, how much time will I have to spend there? Is it worth it, and what would be the sacrifice of being away from my family? Do I really like the person or people with whom I will be working, and will they allow me to be myself when I am in their company? Will this be a mutually satisfying relationship whereby we both learn from each other?

  All of these questions are fair to ask before you have the business. It's best to think these things through before the "game," rather than simply rushing into every situation possible. That way, you are maximizing your chances of long-term success.

Lesson 21

Referral-Selling

Referrals can be the best way to generate new leads. So why don't we receive more referrals and what is the secret to getting more? Before I continue, let me state that this is my opinion. You may not agree, and you don't have to do what I say. This is what has worked for me for more than 20 years. Everyone has a different style and opinion, and I share this information hoping that you will consider giving it a try.

Let me begin by offering a few statistics. The average business speaker or lecturer in the United States delivers approximately 60–75 speeches per year. Since 1991, I have been averaging more than 140 speeches or workshops every year. Here is the best part: I have never made a proactive sales call or asked for a referral. My business has *always* been generated 100-percent by referrals!

What is the secret you ask? There is no one secret, but rather a lot of little steps that got me to this place. Before I start with the steps, let me tell you about someone who totally disagrees with me and is also correct in his approach.

My friend and competitor, Marv Montgomery, is one of the finest sales trainers I have ever known and had the pleasure to work with. He is basically your all-around good guy and a real class act. His training was in retail, and before he went out on his own about 20 years ago, he was the corporate sales trainer for one of the top chains of jewelry stores in the United States.

We debate this point all the time. He teaches a course on referral-selling. He uses it, and it works for him. It works for the people he trains. Marv loves to ask for referrals, and people love to give them to him. Why wouldn't they? He's honest, sincere, classy, always in a good mood, and people are proud to pass along his name. Even though we might not agree on the subject, it works well for him and I say, "If it ain't broke, don't fix it."

Now back to the steps I was referring to earlier. First, regardless of your profession, you must do a good job. That goes without saying. To be the best, it takes hard work and a plan to always be at the top of your game. Whether people want to refer you or you ask for the referral, they have to want to do it. The key word here is *want*. You can't force people to do something they don't want to do. The referral has to be earned.

I believe referrals are similar to doctor recommendations: if people are satisfied with their doctor, they are comfortable referring him or her to other people. Many people don't know where their physician went to school, unless they read the diplomas on the wall out of boredom while waiting for the doctor to enter the examining room. They don't know their doctor's rank in their graduating class. They have no idea what the doctor pays for malpractice insurance. They patronize the doctor because they like and trust him or her, and if they don't spend an unreasonable time sitting around in the waiting room, all the better.

My physician has never asked me for a referral. In fact, no doctor has ever asked me, "Hey, Hal, do you know anybody who could use my services? How about someone with high blood pressure or a bad back? Would you tell him about me, or do you mind if I call him?"

It takes many years for a physician to build a practice. There is no short cut or quick way to get business. The road to a successful practice is through hard work, keeping up-to-date on the latest medical advances, always trying to do the best for every patient, and making the patient comfortable.

Start keeping in touch with your current customers on a regular basis, and see how your referrals increase. Try calling them to ask if everything is going well with the product or service you provided them. This is different from just calling them when you anticipate they are about to run out of the product or service you provide. Calling when you aren't trying to sell something can be a powerful tool in building relationships. It shows you care. I stay in touch with my clients all the time. You've heard the phrase "out of touch, out of mind." I want my clients to remember me. I might even call to refer other speakers to them that I think it will help them reach their business goals. Or, I might just call to say hello. The key is that I am always sincere and interested in what they say. It's my job!

Getting Past the Screen

The screen, such as a receptionist or office administrator, is the key person who determines if you will be successful in reaching the decision-maker with information about your product or service. Most salespeople have no idea how to interact with these gatekeepers whose job it is to decide who will get through and who won't. This can be one of the toughest areas for a salesperson.

Most salespeople haven't been trained in the art of working with a screen or gatekeeper when making cold calls. I can't tell you how many salespeople I have seen who just ramrod their way past the receptionist, trying to see the decision-maker, or even worse, took the sweet-talking approach and thought they were charming the screen. If you were insincere to the screen, and you were also dumb enough to give that person information or your brochure, understand that most likely your information has gone into the wastebasket by the time you open your car door.

Some salespeople talk down to the screen as if he or she were nothing more than an inconvenience. The screen is a person who is trying to do his or her job, and part of that job is to keep you out! If you respect him or her, he or she, in turn, will probably respect you. By being sincere, you will be different from most salespeople, and more important, you will be a person he or she will remember. People will appreciate it if you treat them with courtesy and respect. For example, if you stop by and the screen looks extremely busy, just say, "You look very busy. Would it be better if I came back another time?" If he says yes, get the person's name and call another time. He will remember that you were courteous, and now you've made a friend and not an enemy.

As I have stated many times before, the use of questions is imperative. Your job is not to sell to the screen or to talk about what you do or sell. Your job is to briefly introduce yourself and ask a few questions about the company. After a brief introduction, ask for the decision-maker or whomever they suggest you see. If you start with, "Hi, my name is Hal; who is the decision-maker?" you have just tried to blow past the screen, and he or she will know it.

By the way, if the screen is basically a jerk (or as Fred Flintstone used to say, "Sometimes Wilma, the bone is just too tight") don't fight it. Be smart and call after business hours. The screen will probably be gone. Most decision-makers appreciate a professional salesperson, and one who is calling after standard business hours is dedicated to their job! If they don't want to buy from you, they may try to hire you!

As companies downsize and go to lean operations in both their plants and offices, many companies have eliminated the receptionist position. When you approach a company's entrance, you are greeted by a glassed-in reception area but no one is sitting at the desk. Instead, there is often a phone with which you can call the person you want to see by either entering her extension or her name. If you are on a cold call and haven't done your homework, you are out of luck. No name, no contact. You may be lucky and punch in a random number in the hopes that you can get in through whomever answers the phone. I wouldn't count on it and would always have a back-up plan. (The same applies if you are making cold calls by telephone. If you don't know the person's name or extension you have just eliminated your chances of speaking with a human being.)

How to Sell Like a Pro in Two Minutes

Too many salespeople dance around the table; they don't get to the main point. They talk about nonsense such as the weather or sports. This type of conversation, although it may be considered polite, wastes time and doesn't build true relationships. Remember, it's about asking questions to determine what the customer needs.

I used this idea about 30 years ago, and it worked well at that time: I had a small egg timer that was about one-and-a-half inches tall. When I was in someone's office, whether it was a cold call or an appointment, I told them that by the time the sand ran out (which was six minutes) I would be done with my sales call. Sometimes I told them this on the phone before the appointment, so that they would be more likely to agree to meet. Think about it: who doesn't have six minutes in their day to hear something?

My approach was simple, straight to the point, and honest. For example, when scheduling appointments, I might have said the following, "Hello, my name is Hal Becker, and I work for (fill in company name here). I would like to meet you for no more than six minutes. When the six minutes is up (and you can time me), either

111

you will be interested or you will have learned something new! I won't take more time than I am asking for." When I sat down in their office I pulled out my little egg timer and said, "I would like to ask you three simple questions, and when the sand runs down I will leave as I mentioned to you on the phone." Then I would ask:

1. Are you familiar with our company? If yes, what aspects are you familiar with? If no, why not?

2. Tell me what you like, or perhaps even dislike, about your present supplier or vendor (obviously, my competitor).

3. If you realized that doing business with us would be more beneficial to you, and you wondered why you hadn't considered doing business with our company sooner, would you take a look at us now?

This conversation should take about six minutes, and then I would thank them for their time, ask if I could call them to follow up, and then excuse myself. The person behind the desk was amazed, because I kept my promise. Think about it: if he is interested, he will want to meet me again, and now he can trust me because I kept my promise by keeping to the six-minute deal.

Try it. You'll want to use your own words, style, and whatever questions you want to ask, as long as it gets the other person to talk about him or herself and the company, rather than you just going over your presentation and talking non-stop. By the way, you can always talk about the weather or sports after you get the business relationship established.

Why Salespeople Are Supposed to Cheat

I read a statistic once that said 68 percent of college students cheat at least once during their four-year journey leading to graduation. I did some research and found additional studies that came to the same conclusion.

Once, our local daily newspaper ran an article about creative ways students cheated on an exam. I found the article to be highly unusual and amusing. In one case, a chemistry student brought a plastic bottle of Pepsi and a number two pencil to an exam; both were allowed in the classroom during the test. The night before the exam, he carefully removed the label surrounding the bottle. He then scanned the label including the area where they had the calorie and nutrition information and removed the numbers. In its place he typed in all the answers to his chemistry exam, re-scanned the label, and glued it back on the Pepsi bottle. During the exam, he had the bottle in front of him with all the information he needed to pass the test. The teachers never had a clue!

With all this time and incredible ingenuity, maybe he could have done something else...like actually study for the exam! I do give him credit for the initiative and creativity, although it was very misguided. This kid will probably grow up to be very success-ful and, hopefully, not a chemist at DuPont or work for NASA.

The problem is that kids aren't supposed to cheat. Salespeople, on the other hand, should cheat. What I mean by this statement is that salespeople should be prepared when engaged in their day-to-day activities. Doctors and nurses have a questionnaire that they use during your annual physical. Lawyers have notes that they use during a trial, and teachers have a lesson plan before they even walk into the classroom. Salespeople have brochures or a blank legal pad!

How should salespeople "cheat"? It's a simple and easy quick fix that takes about three to five minutes before any sales call. Before I explain how this is done, I want to mention that on the hundreds of sales calls I have been on during the past 30 years ob-serving people in the field, I rarely see anyone do this:

1. Think of what you want to accomplish during the sales call. Is it to just meet and greet, or to gather in-formation for a second call? Maybe you are trying to establish trust or actually close for an order. The point here is to identify your objective.

2. Write out your questions. Go in prepared and know what you want to ask so you can focus on the client or customer. This allows you to listen to them more effectively, because you are not thinking of what you are going to say next. It also allows you to control the conversation and get the information you feel is nec-essary to provide the right recommendation for the customer.

Most salespeople tell me, "I don't need to write questions down; I have them in my head." I don't buy this reasoning. There is no excuse for not being prepared and demonstrating to the customer or client that you are at the top of your game on every sales call.

For most sales organizations, you can easily put a one-page questionnaire together for fact-finding on the initial call and duplicate this for every customer. If you need to make changes, at best, they will be minor adjustments.

If you start to "cheat" on sales calls by going in prepared with your written questions, not only will your customer be impressed, but you will come out of the sales call having accomplished more than you anticipated. And if you want to bring a Pepsi bottle in with you, please leave it in the car. I'm sure the client will have refreshments!

LESSON 25

Dating and Selling:
Is There a Difference?

Have you ever gone on a date, had a really nice time, and after a day or two, the guy or girl still hasn't called you? You decide to call instead, and leave a voicemail similar to this: "Hey, I had a nice time the other night and would love to get together again. If you feel like calling back, my cell is...." You get the picture.

A couple more days go by, and you hear nothing from this person, so you make a final attempt. You leave another voicemail, saying, "Hey, it's me again, and I thought I would try one more time to see if you would like to get together."

At this point, though it may be annoying to never have found out why the other person isn't interested despite the good date you had, it's probably best to give up, rather than become the stalker who leaves 623 messages.

This is the sales rep's problem. Though it's acceptable to be a little more persistent in sales than you would in a dating situation, many salespeople keep calling the prospect hoping for a return call and soon become a pest. It's always a bad move to do this. The smart thing to do is to dial *67, which blocks the caller ID, and call at different times. When you get your customer on the phone, just say, "Hi, this is Hal, and I'd like to ask you one quick question, and whatever your answer is, I'm fine with it—really! Because we haven't spoken since our last meeting, I was wondering what you thought of the product I was offering. I don't want to be a pest; I am just curious to see what happened."

Either way, you get an answer and hopefully the truth. You need to know that you will never get direct, honest answers unless you can ask direct, honest questions in the first place. When you soften the question by saying that you are curious and you would like to know the real reason, you will probably get a straight answer—not all the time, but it's still better than not knowing and walking away from the situation guessing at what possibly happened. Additionally, with the information you get from customers who haven't called back, you can better understand how to improve your product, service, or sales technique.

Quiz 6

1. When networking or meeting a customer for the first time
   A. Make small talk about sports or the weather.
   B. Ask a question that is sincere and different.
   C. Talk about yourself non-stop.
   D. Tell him that you are a great salesperson and about what you can do to improve his life.

2. With respect to existing customers, you should
   A. Stay in touch often.
   B. Call only once a year.
   C. Never call them unless there is a problem.
   D. Always ask for referrals, no matter what.

3. Great relationships are built by

   A. Having a 30-second elevator speech.

   B. Deciding what relationship you want, then working on it over time.

   C. Going to as many fundraisers as possible and donating money.

   D. Being reactive rather than proactive.

4. Which is the best way to add sales or to bring in more business?

   A. Working with past or existing customers.

   B. Looking for new business by some form of cold calling.

   C. Networking events for additional exposure to meet more people.

   D. All the above.

5. On a cold call, the screen is

   A. A big TV in the lobby.

   B. The secretary or receptionist with whom you first make contact.

   C. There to make you coffee.

   D. Just another inconvenience in your selling day.

6. When you first encounter the screen

    A. Try to get past him or her quickly.

    B. Be as sweet as can be.

    C. Try to bribe him or her with donuts.

    D. Treat him or her as an equal and show respect.

7. If you have no luck getting by the screen

    A. Just walk past them anyway.

    B. Bring more donuts.

    C. Call during lunch or after business hours.

    D. Come back later that day.

8. Before you go on a sales call you should

    A. Go to the bathroom.

    B. Wash your car.

    C. Have a glass of wine.

    D. Write out your questions.

9. Most salespeople say

    A. I don't have to write the questions down, I have them in my head.

    B. I'm good enough, I'm smart enough, and, gosh darn it, people like me.

    C. Selling is easy to do, because I like being around people.

    D. I hate my sales manager; she should just leave me alone.

10. If you have your questions written down in front of you during the sales call, the customer will be

    A. Looking at you like you are a real loser.

    B. Impressed.

    C. Happy and want to start to dance.

    D. Inviting you to their next barbecue.

Cold Calls, Phone Selling, and Other Contact Options

"At least you're getting your foot in the door, Dave!"

Cartoon © Priyanka Pai. Used with permission.

LESSON 26

Cold Calls, Phone Calls, and E-mail

A *great* salesperson is on top of his or her game, which essentially comes down to two areas: One is the constant awareness of existing clients and making sure they stay customers by keeping in touch. The other is the consistent effort to obtain new business. This section will explore obtaining new business through phone sales and cold calling.

A cold call occurs when someone knocks on the door of a business without an appointment. Typically, this is best done in a geographic territory where the salesperson can do multiple calls in a given day without burning himself out. A nice, round number is 10 to 20 calls a day. Check lesson 19 for how to get past the screen.

Though each salesperson has his or her unique personality, especially on a cold call, the objective is always the same: to introduce yourself and request permission to spend a few minutes asking questions about the business to see whether your product or service is a good fit. If it is, you spend a little time going over the benefits and try to set up another appointment.

Yes, that is correct. Go for another appointment. Remember, your whole goal in selling is to build relationships. Most people are busy and have other things to do besides sitting around and waiting for salespeople to show up and interrupt their day. Be conscious of their time and respect it. If there is an interest, the prospect will want to set up another appointment, will be impressed that you have good people skills, and will want you to come back for a formal meeting. When you do return for the scheduled appointment, the prospect will be expecting you, and you will both be fully prepared.

The beauty of cold calls is that you have no idea what will happen next. Sometimes, everything you do turns to gold and the next day everything does not. It is simply a game, and the numbers will eventually work in your favor.

Cold phone calls are similar to in-person cold calls. The goal here is the same: to get the appointment. You are not trying to close the deal over the telephone. Once again, the client is not expecting your phone call. Here's the bottom line: have your agenda in front of you and get to the point. People don't want to chit-chat unless there is *something* to chitchat about. If you are going to schmooze, do it after the sales call and make sure the topic is of interest to your prospect.

Here are some points to consider:

- If your territory is Utah and you live in Cleveland, the phone is a good idea.

- It is easier to hang up the phone than to kick you out of an office on a cold call, so you may be able to make more of an impact in person.

- The phone will allow you to do more calls in a given time, but it is harder to establish a rapport.

- Within any specific amount of time, you can't get as many cold calls done as you would phone calls. However, cold calls are better at building a relationship by being there and noticing the surroundings.

Almost everyone is now available by e-mail, and it's easy to get anyone's e-mail, even the CEO of a company! E-mail is great for a quick response or for a question to which you need an answer. You can use brief e-mail to set up an appointment, but it shouldn't be used for an ongoing conversation that you can have more effectively in person.

Drawbacks of e-mail include unpublished listings and spam accounts that block unknown users. The prospect also has the option of deleting your e-mail without even reading it. One option to dealing with this is to go to your prospect's Website. Almost every Website has a "contact us" section. If all else fails, use this feature and carefully craft your message, making sure you ask that it be directed to the person who makes the decisions.

In short, e-mail works well for quick exchanges of information, but it shouldn't replace in-person relationships, which is the ideal way to acquire and keep customers.

LESSON 27

Why Scripts Don't Work

I am still amazed that companies continue to train their salespeople to use scripts when making telephone sales. Scripts have almost never worked and almost never will. The very modest success you may have achieved with scripts is nothing compared to what you would have found using a finely tuned questionnaire.

When I say "scripts," I am talking about the rigid text on a piece of paper or computer screen that tells the salesperson what to say, what to offer, who her company is, and so on. People can spot this one-sided type of conversation, and have never wanted it and never will. Who wants to listen to someone read from a script? Script selling isn't old school or new school; it's just wrong!

Here's an example of the type of ineffective telephone sales call that some companies actually think works. This type of call is made by small companies as well as large Fortune 100 companies that continue to use it as part of their sales tactics. This example actually happened to one of my friends, a national training director for one of the largest jewelry store chains in the United States.

He received a call, the voice saying, "Hello, my name is Debbie, and I am from ABC Chimney Sweep Company, and we have a special today. It is only $35, and we come out to clean your chimney, oil the parts inside, put a screen on top of your chimney to protect you from birds or squirrels coming inside your house, and we will give you a total inspection for only $35."

My friend Marv said, "Hey, that sounds great, but what kind of special do you have for me if I don't have a chimney?" Pretty funny, huh? Instead, the call should have gone like this. "Hello, my name is Debbie and I am from ABC Chimney Sweep Company and I would like to ask you two or three quick questions and it will not take more than 45 seconds, I promise!"

Marv says, "Sure, okay." Debbie now asks, "Do you have a chimney?" If Marv answers yes, the next question would be, "When was the last time you had it cleaned?" If the answers warrant additional conversation, Debbie could then describe the special she can offer.

The best conversations are two-way, not one-sided. Get the customer to talk by asking questions and getting information from him or her. That is *how to sell*. People don't want to be sold to or forced into buying; they want to be helped and to feel they are getting something that is either of value or makes them better.

Believe it or not, *most* companies sell incorrectly over the phone. They think what they are doing is right, but it isn't. Most of the managers who set up these scripts aren't well trained in the science of sales to begin with. They think that they are until you ask the manager what books on sales he or she has read lately, or what courses have they taken during the last year.

Here's an example of one of the only phone calls I received from a salesperson at a mobile windshield repair company, who introduced himself and asked if he could ask me one quick question: "Do you have any chips or cracks in your windshield?" If my answer was no, he was done! My answer was yes, I have a chip. They now said, "If we could come to your place of business or home and repair it for $40, would you be interested?" My chip is gone.

LESSON 28

Make It a Game

You should have fun every day while selling. People love to laugh, and most people have a good sense of humor. It's important to incorporate appropriate, friendly humor and fun into sales calls each day. Author Robert Shook seems to agree. Some years back, he wrote a book titled, *I'll Get Back to You*. It contained 156 ways of guaranteeing people would return your phone call.

Here are some techniques I used more than 20 years ago. When I couldn't get people to return my calls, I sent them a fax and asked them to pick one reason they didn't call back:

- You lost my messages and forgot to call back.

- You are just not interested.

- You hoped I would just give up and go away.

- You are on vacation for a long, long time.

Most people got a chuckle out of this because it was different, and called me back or faxed back for me to call them. We then started on a different course because we both had something in common: the ability to laugh.

Here are a few ideas you can try that are fun and different. Some are in Shook's book and they still work today:

1. A few years ago, I met this big, burly guy of 275 pounds, an ex-linebacker but a nice, sweet guy. He bought Valentine's Day cards similar to the ones third-graders would send to their friends in school and mailed them to his clients or prospects as a way to keep in touch.

2. If you are dealing with an organization that makes everything complicated, and its people blame it on the red tape in their company, buy a roll of red tape, unroll it, and pack it into a ball. Then send it to the company with a note, "Now that we've gone through all the red tape..."

3. Do you ever have a customer or prospect that offers to call you back but doesn't? Around Halloween buy a couple of small, plastic skeletons and little coffins. Place a skeleton in a coffin, and send it with a note saying, "This is me waiting for you to call back."

Lesson 29

The Video Idea

Once in a while I come across an idea that makes so much sense that it's kind of scary that I didn't think of it sooner. When you finish reading this chapter it will set you back about $150, but it will be well worth it. My small investment has already made me more than 100 times the purchase price, and that's no exaggeration. Here's the story of how I accidentally got this great idea.

Several years ago for my birthday my wife gave me a mini camcorder, now called digital video camcorders. A flip camera or smart phone that records in HD (high definition) and fits into the palm of your hand will do. It is truly one of the best gadgets I own.

When you get a new toy like this you want to find creative ways to use it. Some of my friends were reuniting a band that played in the 1970s, and its leader decided to take the helm and put a show together. They wanted all original members, so they could honestly say it was a reunion of the whole band. Unfortunately, their drummer had passed away. To make matters worse, their second drummer who played with them for more than four years was in a serious car accident a couple of months before the concert was

132

planned. The venue was an outdoor amphitheater that held a few thousand people, and they were expecting to fill the place.

Part of me was serious and the other part was just kidding around trying to have fun with my new toy. I put one of their songs on my stereo, and I played my drums along with the song while my friend recorded me. We decided to e-mail it to one of our mutual friends who would get a kick out of it. What I didn't expect is that my friend would forward the e-mail to the band leader, and he was impressed enough to invite me to do the show with the other band members. They wanted to use me because I played with the band once in the 1970s, which enabled them to say that they had all original members playing in the band. Naturally, the program gave a tribute to the two other drummers.

I had to tell this story to set up this great idea. It struck me in the shower one day I could use the digital recorder to record personalized videos that were less than 30 seconds long and e-mail them to a few select people that could use my services.

I had a list of four companies that were on the fence as to whether they should use me to train their sales forces and management teams. I had my office manager hold the camera and tape me in my office. All four videos took about 10 minutes to shoot and the same amount of time to e-mail. Within a short time, I had heard back from three of the companies, and two agreed to work with me. Obviously, the idea worked, and it was a fun and easy project to accomplish.

If you decide to try something like this, you need to keep a few basic points in mind:

1. Keep the video short, right to the point, and less than 45 seconds long.

2. Keep the material you are recording light and airy. Don't close hard for the business.

3. Make it fun and focus on the benefit they will receive from doing business with you.

4. Be creative. You will be remembered for your originality.

LESSON 30

Selling Top Down

Salespeople usually take the course of least resistance. In other words, we don't want to hear the word *no*. So what do we do? Stretch out the selling cycle, see the wrong people, avoid the real issues, and even stop asking questions. We do all this to avoid the no and to keep the prospect alive in our minds. It blows me away as a sales trainer that most salespeople are still afraid of the no.

There are many qualities that make the sales pros different from the rest. One of the basics is that they get to the right decision-maker. The key word here is "right." I have always had this little line as a motto: "I will never take a no from someone who can't say yes."

The first question you ask to the person you have identified as the company decision-maker is this: "Is there anyone else who participates in the decision-making process with you?" Perhaps the company makes decisions by committee, through a board of directors, or by a contracted buyer. You won't know the answer until you ask the question.

Now for the good stuff. (I wish I knew this 25 years ago when I was actually selling in the field.) People who were older than me or people who had positions of power and authority always intimidated me. The older I get, however, the more I realize that we are all the same. In fact, a lot of these "power people" just married into the family or just happened to be born with the last name that was also on the building. Some people reached their position by being in the right place at the right time. Others got there by being smart, working hard, and earning their position and title.

So what should you do? Avoid these powerful people? No, you should start *top down*. Yes, that's right; you go all the way to the top of the heap, or, in this case, the company.

Here's an example of what you can do: First, call the CEO's office and speak to her administrative assistant. Say, "Hi, my name is Hal and I would like to ask you just one quick question; it will only take a few seconds. Who is the person responsible for making the decisions in _____ area?" Now you have the name and, hopefully, the direct dial phone number. Next, phone the decision-maker and *do not* leave a voicemail message to return your call if you don't reach him. It is *not* his responsibility to return your phone call. You are the one who is making the sales call. If you reach him, say, "Hi, my name is Hal. I was talking to Ms. Jones' office, and it was suggested that I give you a call. I would like to ask you a few questions that will take no longer than 75 seconds. Is this a good time?"

Keep it simple, upbeat, and fun. Remember, your goal is not to sell over the phone, but to pique the decision-maker's interest by asking a few questions and getting the appointment. Repeat, *your goal is to get the appointment, not make the sale over the phone.* Remember the decision-maker is not expecting your first call. Is it beneficial for him to listen further or even meet you? Forget about what you want; what does he want? Being respectful of his needs will make it even more likely that you'll get an appointment with him.

LESSON 31

Think Prospects

Too many salespeople worry about the number of their monthly sales. The salesperson can feel happy when he or she had a good month, but at the same time worry about what will happen next month. The same is true for the sales managers. Despite good months, they are always looking ahead to the future and worrying about whether the good results will continue and how to guarantee that they do. This phenomenon happens regardless of the type of business.

The key to long-term success is to quit thinking about sales. A sale is a short-term goal and focuses on the present. I like to believe in long-range goals. Focusing on the future keeps things more consistent over the long haul.

Let's look at it from a statistical approach. Study after study shows that in business-to-business selling situations, salespeople usually close between 50 and 70 percent of their legitimate prospects. That means the customer was ready to make a decision. Who they will buy from, what they will spend, and when they will make the decision is what qualifies that person as a genuine prospect. With that in mind, if a salesperson has four prospects in a given month, that would equate to having approximately two successful sales towards his performance quota. Let's assume he needs four sales that month to be at his quota of 100 percent. He is now at 50 percent of his plan.

I remember when I was just starting out as a salesperson and working at Xerox. We had to sell five copiers per month (these were the smaller units) to be at 100 percent of our sales goals. Everyone wanted to reach 250 percent, because if they achieved that goal, they received a high bonus for that quarter. If they continued that 250-percent performance for the other three quarters, or the whole year, they also received additional quarterly bonuses and a substantial year-end bonus. The big goal, and income, to achieve when I was a sales rep for Xerox was to be at 250 percent of plan or better.

To me, it was simple to set up my sales goals. If selling five copiers put me at 100 percent, then I would need to sell at least 14 copiers to get me over 250 percent. Not an easy task to do, but it could be done with a consistent game plan that included making many more sales calls over the year.

Using the numbers I discussed before and figuring a 50 percent close rate, I would need 28 to 30 prospects per month. I like round numbers, so let's use 30. It was that simple! I now had a game plan that I could manage and stick with. It was simple, straight to the point, and something that, in order to reach my goals, I could not deviate from. I decided to concentrate on *the prospects, not the sale*, and by doing this on a continuous basis, the sales naturally followed.

Let me tell you, that plan worked. The sales were better than I expected. I was well above 300 percent for the year and was far ahead of the other salespeople in revenue generated for the company.

It was a very simple trick. I quit thinking about sales and concentrated at keeping my prospect base at 30 legitimate customers who were ready or fairly close to making a decision. Staying in touch with my current prospects and continually adding new ones meant there wasn't going to be a slump in my sales. No spikes or bell curves, just a nice easy flow of sales that produced even sales all year long. Quit thinking about the month when you should care about the year.

[ACTION STEP]

Here's an aid that will help you keep your prospects organized:

- What predominant methods of prospecting are you currently using to build your business?

- Which prospects will you call this week?

- Which past customers will you call this week?

- Which current customers will you call this week?

LESSON 32

Call Me After the 1st!

"Call me after the 1st!" Every December, these are the words most often heard by salespeople. It's almost like a ritual; you know it's coming, but you hope that your ears won't hear the sounds. Most salespeople reply, "Sure, I'll call you on such and such a day."

Do not do that! Yes, you heard me. Don't cave in and whimper out of the office or off the phone like a beaten puppy. Do the right thing and act like a professional salesperson. Your job is to help the customer if you can, and sometimes that might mean doing something different.

Don't get me wrong. If the customer is in the retail business and this is her busiest time of the year, naturally you will abide by her wishes and call back when things slow down. For most businesses or industries, however, this is an especially slow time of the year, even more so the last two weeks of the month. This could be a huge advantage for you!

First, you have to remember that no one likes a pushy salesperson, so use common sense and know when to back off or if you are upsetting the customer. The key is to be sincere and to create a win-win situation for both parties. As I've mentioned before, great salespeople do not talk; they ask questions to either discover information or to get their point across to the customer. This is no different.

In the situation where the customer is trying to put you off (that is what he is doing unless he is truly busy or the timing is just bad), you need to discover the true picture of what is happening. This can easily be accomplished with one or two questions or suggestions. They are as follows:

- "Mr. or Ms. Customer, after the holidays, I assume you'll get busy again and try to kick the New Year off with a great start, is that correct?"

- "If we can meet for 10 to 12 minutes sometime before January 1st, and you find interest in our product or service, then you can call me at your convenience if this fits your needs. Would that be okay?"

- "If this time of the year is a little slower, it might be a great time to meet for just a few minutes so you can think about what product or service we provide would work best for you."

By asking a few simple questions, you just turned things around to where you are in charge of the conversation, and now you will get a better idea if he can meet with you or not. If he can't, don't worry. You did your best to see if an appointment would work for both of your schedules.

By trying to be a little more proactive in your sales approach during the holiday season, you might find a little more reward in the number of appointments you have compared with previous years. Don't be afraid to ask these questions mentioned. Just be conscious of the fine line between great salesmanship and being too aggressive or obnoxious.

[ACTION STEP]

List of prospects I will call this week.

1. Name: Phone #:

2. Name: Phone #:

3. Name: Phone #:

4. Name: Phone #:

5. Name: Phone #:

6. Name: Phone #:

7. Name: Phone #:

8. Name: Phone #:

9. Name: Phone #:

10. Name: Phone #:

List of past customers I will call this week.

1. Name: Phone #:

2. Name: Phone #:

3. Name: Phone #:

4. Name: Phone #:

5. Name: Phone #:

6. Name: Phone #:

7. Name: Phone #:

8. Name: Phone #:

9. Name: Phone #:

10. Name: Phone #:

List of current customers I will call this week.

1.   Name: Phone #:

2.   Name: Phone #:

3.   Name: Phone #:

4.   Name: Phone #:

5.   Name: Phone #:

6.   Name: Phone #:

7.   Name: Phone #:

8.   Name: Phone #:

9.   Name: Phone #:

10. Name: Phone #:

Quiz 7

1. A cold call is

    A. Calling someone for the first time.

    B. Calling someone during winter months.

    C. The term used when you get the cold shoulder from someone.

    D. Making calls on someone when you don't feel well.

2. A smart salesperson will make

    A. One to two new calls per day.

    B. Three to five new calls per day.

    C. 10-20 new calls per day.

    D. As many as you can before your voice gives out.

3. On a cold call you should

    A. Be prepared for a no.

    B. Be prepared for a yes.

    C. Have no idea what will happen next.

    D. All of the above.

4. On a cold call, if you get to see the decision-maker, you should ask for

    A. 2 hours with coffee and donuts.

    B. 3-5 minutes.

    C. No specific time.

    D. 15-20 minutes.

5. The object of the cold call is to

    A. Sell them on the spot.

    B. Just introduce yourself.

    C. Set up a future appointment if there is a need.

    D. Badmouth your competition.

6. When making a video to send to a client or prospect

    A. Keep it short and right to the point.

    B. Pack as much material as you can in a 5-minute video.

    C. Be very detailed and very serious.

    D. Always use an experienced director so this becomes a mini-movie.

7. When making this little video

    A. Make it fun.

    B. Focus on the benefit the client will receive from the video.

    C. Do not close hard for the business.

    D. All the above.

8. Great salespeople sell to

    A. The receptionist.

    B. Whoever they get an audience with.

    C. The easiest person to talk to.

    D. The right decision-maker.

9. The best salespeople

    A. Sell to purchasing agents and buyers.

    B. Start top down.

    C. Work middle management.

    D. Will only sell the top person.

10. When you get the name of the proper contact

    A. Say the CEO insisted you talk to him.

    B. Identify yourself by quoting the CEO.

    C. Say you are the CEO's cousin.

    D. Identify yourself as being referred by the CEO's office.

11. Many salespeople will
    A. Sell only one of their company's products.
    B. Stretch out the selling cycle so they do not hear no.
    C. Sell only on Mondays and Thursdays.
    D. Only sell to people that have a lot of money.

Time Management

"Look folks, when I talk about time management, I mean spending more time selling—not golfing or shopping!"

Cartoon © Margaret Li. Used with permission.

The 15-Minute Plan

Everyone in the business sector can be better at time management. I've attended at least eight courses on time management, and they were all helpful in their own way. But nothing will be as effective as this simple idea.

Spend a week examining how you spend your time. Make a copy for each day of the work week of the calendar on pages 152–154. It divides each day into 15-minute increments. Starting with Monday (or whenever your week starts), each day write down what you did in the time that corresponds on the calendar. For example, at 7:30 a.m. you left and drove to work. When you got to the office, let's assume that you went through your e-mails from 8:30 until 9:15 a.m. Continue to do this all week, recording everything that you do during the day.

At the end of the week, review how you spent your time. You might be amazed at what you see. Some things you might be able to delegate; some things you might not need to do anymore. Maybe you are spending too much time in the car driving to appointments when you could schedule them in a more organized fashion. You can look at your day or week and adjust your schedule to improve your organization.

This exercise is simple and powerful, if you take the time to do it and be honest with yourself about the time that you're wasting. With this new knowledge, you will be more organized and better prepared to plan your productive day.

[ACTION STEP]

Day Planner

Date:
7 A.M.
8 A.M.
9 A.M.
10 A.M.

11 A.M.
12 P.M.
1 P.M.
2 P.M.
3 P.M.
4 P.M.
5 P.M.

6 P.M.

7 P.M.

Task List / Notes

Manage a Territory Like a Bus Tour

If you ever go on a vacation to a city with multiple tourist attractions, a great option is to take one of those tour buses. My favorite things in New York City are the double-decker buses. The reason I bring up sightseeing is that the tour operator has every last detail planned before you board the bus. Whether it's a quick, two-hour tour of Central Park, Times Square, the Empire State Building, and a few other attractions, or a day-long option with many stops, the buses don't just randomly drive around the city.

A sightseeing tour starts with destination A and then goes to B, C, and so on. The tour is planned down to the smallest detail with the shortest amount of driving time between distances. Obviously, they do this to pack as much as they can into the tour, while at the same time saving fuel and wear and tear on the vehicle. They study routes and traffic patterns, and review feedback from prior passengers regarding what they liked and didn't like. The intended result is a satisfied customer.

Why bring this up in a book on sales? Simple! A salesperson should do the same thing. He or she needs to think like a tour operator going on a sightseeing trip. Instead of the sights, the sales rep should think of clients and prospects to call on. Most sales-people don't have well-planned days. They just work with a few scheduled appointments and don't give much thought to what the rest of the day will bring or how they can be most effective.

Too many times I've seen a salesperson visit a client, then drive to another zip code just to make some cold calls. This is a waste of time. The sales rep might think that he is working, but he is not really accomplishing anything. Just because a salesperson spends time out of the office does not necessarily mean he is working with great execution or effective time management. The more "windshield time" a salesperson spends, the less time he is in front of a customer getting a yes or even a no. The key to a busy, successful day in the "field" is to do as much as possible in the shortest amount of time. The more people you see in a given day, the better the opportunity to improve your chances of selling something new and retaining your client base.

For example, if you have a 9 a.m. appointment in a certain area or zip code in a city, try to stay there for as long as you can making cold calls or visiting other clients nearby until your next appointment. If you are well prepared, your next appointment (let's say at 11:00 a.m.) is in the same zip code, and you can continue to make calls in the same area without driving any lengthy distances.

LESSON 35

A Day in the Life of...

Great salespeople do things differently. They want to succeed and have a better road map to their destination, which is indicative of all true professionals who are at the top of their game. This isn't a once in a while event or occurrence, but rather something that's done consistently throughout their careers.

We all know that many of the traits a great salesperson possesses can't be trained. On the other hand, there are numerous characteristics than can be learned and put into practice. The key is to make these practices a habit and to do them on a regular basis.

Here is a typical day of a top salesperson in the world of business-to-business.

- **Morning routine:** Start the day off with something that's refreshing. Take time for a great workout or a soothing cup of coffee. It should set the tone for the next 8 to 10 hours. During your drive to the office, you can prepare in your mind what needs to be accomplished that day.

- **Time in the office:** When you arrive at the office, what do you do? You might spend some time talking to other people. If you do converse with them, remember to be sincere. Too many salespeople just do the "Hey, can you do me a favor?" A good team is made up of great people working together to achieve a common goal. The productive time in the office is looking at the information you need for that day. Do you have all the necessary data for the clients you are going to see that day? Are the call reports up-to-date so you can see what has transpired recently? Make copies and take them with you or make sure your laptop or other electronic device has all the current data.

- **Pre-call planning:** Before you go into the client or prospect's office, ask yourself if you are really ready to go in there. What do you want to accomplish today? Do you have your questions written out? Let me emphasize that, because it's so important and too few salespeople actually take the two to three minutes to do this extremely important exercise. Write out the questions you want to ask or the subjects you want to cover so you can stay focused on the objective of the sales call.

- **Actual sales call:** This is where the real action takes place, the one or two hours of each day that will truly make a difference. The great salesperson gets right to the point. There is no need to talk about weather or sports, unless you already know the person and this is something that he or she likes to discuss. Look at your notes and get down to business. Isn't that why you're there in the first place? You can discuss unimportant issues that have nothing to do with the sales call after the call. Stick to your agenda and find out her needs instead of talking about what you want to sell.

- **Post-call organization:** Did you update the records? Be on top of your game here by always keeping good notes. You'll thank yourself in the future when it comes time to call on this company again. The professional salesperson has a detailed account of what happens on every call, so the information is always there for the salesperson or anyone else who might need it. If you promised the prospect or client something, are you on top of it? Is it written down so you don't forget? The great salesperson *always* keeps her promises, big or small!

- **Getting ready for the rest of the day:** Let's assume that you have successfully completed your first call of the morning. Is the rest of your day lined up in a similar fashion? Do you have at least two or three appointments per day? When you go home at night, do you truly feel that your day was productive and a great use of your time, or were you just going through the motions? The great salesperson fills in the time between appointments with phone calls or maybe even a few cold calls.

The typical day described here isn't a once in a while thing. It's the daily blueprint for a salesperson's career. The more time spent doing the right things will determine the way he is viewed by his customers, prospects, and coworkers. Too many average salespeople are happy to reach their quota and then go home for the rest of the day, week, or even month. To be a pro, you must do the things a pro does, each and every day!

[ACTION STEP]

Fill out the following information to get an idea of how you spend your time.

1. Number of appointments per week:

2. Number of existing calls per week:

3. Number of prospecting calls per week:

4. Closing-for-a-sale appointments per week:

Quiz 8

1. Time management is a must for salespeople
   A. Because it allows you to be in front of as many decision-makers as possible.
   B. Because it allows you to work less hours per week.
   C. Because working long days will impress your boss.
   D. Until you get enough clients.

2. It's best to break your day down by
   A. One-hour increments.
   B. 30-minute increments.
   C. Morning and afternoon.
   D. 15-minute increments.

3. The purpose of the time management exercise is to

    A. Look at the time you waste during your day.

    B. Look to see how much time you spent with decision-makers.

    C. Find out how much time you spend driving around.

    D. All of the above.

4. Your day's appointments and cold calls ideally should be with customers in the same

    A. Industry.

    B. Geographical area.

    C. Civic organization.

    D. Page in the phone book.

Handling Objections

"Harry, our new salesperson Jon can handle any objection, don't you agree?"

Cartoon © Bobbie MacDougal. Used with permission.

Jumping Hurdles

Picture a track event with athletes running the hurdles. To win, they must successfully jump over all the hurdles. Likewise, when you jump over all the hurdles you face in a sales call, you complete the race and might even win.

When the objections (the hurdles you face) are answered satisfactorily, you are likely to get the sale. Understand that if the customer is satisfied with your response to the objections, the customer will be buying without much more effort from you. In fact, you will find that you probably won't even have to close the sale because the customer will do it for you.

Believe it or not, objections are a key factor in any sale. Many components go into a sale and the objection phase is an important area that can lead to a successful sale, or at the least, to knowing why you didn't get the sale. An objection is resistance, regardless of the type of sales call or the situation you are in. There are rules to follow regarding objections. Foremost among them is going back to the science of selling and understanding that questions are everything (meaning you should quit talking so much trying to present your case). Let's get started on what to do and what to look for in the course of making a sale.

When a customer appears to be unreceptive to your product, you will find that he usually has a specific objection. Some customer's objections are difficult to answer; others are easy. In any case, a customer's objections are perfectly natural, and meeting them successfully is a fundamental part of selling. You can turn these objections into valuable "sales tools" by recognizing them for what they really are: plain and simple requests for assistance. Consider the following. When customers object to buying, it can mean:

- They are sincere in voicing what they feel is a real reason for not buying.

- They are covering up the real reason for not wanting to buy.

- They are making random objections to buy themselves some time to think it over.

- They do not understand the benefits you are trying to sell and are simply asking for more information.

In each of these instances, the customer is requesting assistance. He is asking you to give him a reason to buy. His specific objection tells you what to say next to bring about his buying decision.

LESSON 37

Obstacle Envy

Learn to love objections and realize that without an objection, a sale is probably not going to be made. If you and the customer are sitting together and the customer isn't saying anything, just give up and quit. But when a customer brings up an objection, it means the customer is showing the first stage of interest in your service or product. People usually think of why they should not buy before they think about buying. They just don't say, "Hey, whatever you're selling I'm buying." If that happens, you better call the bank to check for insufficient funds on the check, because something is wrong.

Follow the customer's objection with a question. Let's say the customer says you are too expensive. Respond with a question, such as, "What did you expect the price to be?"

Some sales trainers or managers train you to say, "I understand how you feel. Many people have felt the same way, and we find this blah, blah, blah." Is that how you would talk to your best friend? I doubt it. Be real. Be the kind of person that you want to buy from, not some "slick dude" with phony rhetoric. It's great to be empathetic, but sometimes getting right to the answer means the customer is more likely to hear your response.

The following techniques will help you deal with objections:

- Be prepared for objections, so you are not caught off guard.

- Never completely ignore the customer's objection.

- Be relaxed while dealing with an objection.

- Determine the real objection by listening carefully to the customer.

- Clarify by paraphrasing, so you understand the objection. Restate the objection in your own words to avoid any misunderstanding.

- Probe deeper into the objections by asking key questions.

- Allow the customer to talk without interruption. Sometimes people talk themselves out of an objection.

- If the objection is vague, translate the vague terms into understandable issues.

- Convince the customer you understand how he/she feels.

- It is not necessary to agree with a customer's objection. Never allow an objection to develop into an argument.

- Have the ability to acknowledge and to counter objections.

- Develop a positive attitude regarding objections rather than displaying fear or irritability.

- The best way to handle an objection is to listen politely and show empathy.

- Be attentive, not defensive.

LESSON 38

Snow White and the Seven Objections

There are really only about seven objections to learn. Let's go through them and the responses you might give the customer:

1. **Objection:** Price- or budget-related issue.

    Response: What were you planning on spending?

2. **Objection:** Let me think about it.

    Response: What do you want to think about?

3. **Objection:** I used you in the past and had a poor experience.

    Response: What was the problem?

4. **Objection:** I need to talk to my boss, or I am not the decision-maker.

    Response: May I talk to him or her directly?

5. **Objection:** I am happy with my current vendor.

    Response: What are you happy with?

6. **Objection:** Delivery time is too slow.

    Response: When do you need it by and why so fast?

7. **Objection:** I need a certain product that you don't carry.

    Response: Would you be willing to try a similar item and give me your opinion?

These are only examples. You have to add your style and personality to your questions and responses so they become yours. Try new things, be creative, and test the waters a little. Remember, you can't sell everyone or answer every objection all the time. Just do the best you can. Your goal is to satisfy the customer the best way possible.

LESSON 39

Role-Play and Passing on Objections

Here is an effective way you can practice dealing with objections. It's also fun. Get your staff together: sales, other managers, support staff, technical. Start the ball rolling with a common objection, such as "It's too expensive." Have everyone write down, in just a couple lines, how he or she responds to that objection, then pass the response to the next person, who reads it to the group.

You'll find yourself saying, "Wow, I like the way she said that." The content may be similar to yours, but you like the way it's packaged. You'll discover, by the way, that you often get the freshest ideas from new people.

Here's a similar exercise you can do that will allow you to examine the objections you face, as well as your replies.

[ACTION STEP]

List the objections you typically encounter and your responses.

Objection #1:

Response:

Objection #2:

Response:

Objection #3:

Response:

Objection #4:

Response:

Objection #5:

Response:

Objection #6:

Response:

Quiz 9

1. Objections are

    A. A salesperson's nightmare.

    B. Necessary in a sale.

    C. Not necessary in a sale.

    D. Something to avoid if possible.

2. When faced with an objection

    A. Run like hell.

    B. Talk about the features and benefits.

    C. Restate the objection in the form of a question.

    D. Try to close the sale and ignore the objection.

3. How many possible objections are there in the world
    of sales?

    A. Unlimited.

    B. About 7.

    C. 100 plus.

    D. 8,321.

4. When it comes to handling objections you should

    A. Act stiff and professional.

    B. Be slick and polished.

    C. Use your own style and personality.

    D. Stick to the hard selling.

5. By discussing objections with your staff, you will find

    A. No one knows how to handle them.

    B. Your company is overwhelmed with
        negative feedback.

    C. You are the only one who knows how to
        handle objections.

    D. Interesting or effective ways your colleagues
        handle objections.

Setting Goals

"By setting our sales goals after the sales, we're able to consistently maintain an above-average sales quota."

Cartoon © Margaret Li. Used with permission.

Why Goals Are Important

You've heard it before and it's true, true, true: a goal without a plan is only a wish. Most people wish for things to happen instead of planning for them to happen. You have to plan how you are going to reach your goals, whether it's buying a house, getting a job, or increasing your sales by 20 percent. Your plan sets you apart from the competition because it's unique to you.

The first step in reaching your goals is to consider your own needs and wants within the organization so you can achieve personal satisfaction from what you are doing. Can't you always tell the person who's in a job he can't stand? He may feel stuck with no other prospects for employment, and he's only there to get the paycheck at the end of the week. If these people also happen to be in sales, it's easy for their unhappiness to spread to the prospect. The second step is to determine the organization's needs and wants so you achieve what the boss considers important.

Look at your sales call goal. Could you make 10 calls a day? Are you too busy to do that? Are you doing really well? Are you happy with the income you are producing? If you'd like to do better, then the only way to do that is to sell more, and the only way to do that is to get more prospects. Look at that as a goal and get busy making a plan.

You will be surprised how much more work you can get done in a given day when you manage the goals you set for yourself. If this is an area where you need improvement, there are many books, seminars, or information on the Internet that will help you. Look at the best salespeople you know. They are goal-oriented.

We've already covered time management. Now it's time to share some key ideas on goal-setting. You can find a lot of ways to make shortcuts. You can streamline your client calls. If you want to get the most results out of your work day, start work at 7 a.m. and work until 6 p.m. Yes, you are putting in long hours. You most likely have other things in your life that are more important than your job. Your family comes first, and that's the way it should be, but to be a successful salesperson, you must put in the adequate time and effort to accomplish your goals.

I find that I can do work-related tasks at times other than when I'm at the office. For instance, I don't do quotes or proposals during the day. I do them at night while I am watching television. You have to study your own day. What are you doing? Every office has paperwork. What paperwork is necessary? Some salespeople spend 50 percent of their time on sales and 50 percent on paperwork. That's not very productive. Set your goals as to where and when you will do sales calls and paperwork.

If you can increase the time you spend in front of decision-makers by 20 percent, you can increase your income and your company's income proportionally. If you can find just 15 more minutes in each day to get in front of a decision-maker, that totals an hour and a half in a week! Now that's a goal that we can all set.

We all have habits. Make sure your habits are productive and work toward your goals. What works for the early birds doesn't work for the night owls and vice versa. If something works well for you, leave it alone; don't change it. Just become as productive as you can while still maintaining a work/life balance.

Setting Goals

Salespeople need to set goals. The following are some ideas to help you in your goal-setting, including why they are necessary.

In setting goals, keep in mind that every goal must meet four criteria, which you can apply to your personal goals as well:

1. It has a specific time frame (days, weeks or months).

2. It is measurable (so you know when you've achieved it).

3. It is realistic (so you don't get frustrated and give up).

4. It is challenging (so you have a sense of accomplishment).

Let's say an average sale is $1,000 and my goal is to make $10,000 more in the coming year. This isn't my company's quota; it's the goal I set for myself. To get this $10,000, I need 10 new clients. I know that if I make 500 cold calls, 25 of those prospects will be interested and 10 will buy and become my new clients.

I need to make 500 cold calls. Figuring on 200 workdays in a year, I would need to make 2.5 additional cold calls a day, or 2 one day and 3 the next. This is how to determine what it will take to reach a sales goal. It's just like working out. You have to set your goals and then carry them out if you want to actually achieve them. How many people actually work out 3 or 4 times a week to get the great body they want? Very few!

Most of us don't like to admit that we are being weak when we take the course of least resistance. The only way to reach your goal is to break it down into bite-size pieces. You have to do a little bit every day. If you ever watched the movie with Bill Murray titled *What About Bob?*, you are familiar with "baby steps." These are essential for the professional salesperson. All this breaks down to is doing a little bit each day and not trying to overload your life. That's how anything gets done from the smallest to the biggest job, including sales. If you don't translate your quota into a daily plan, then after the 25th of the month, you'll be like the many salespeople who scramble and make frantic calls to meet the company's quota. Why do the top salespeople always go over the company quota? There are two reasons: 1) they are working harder than everyone else, and 2) they are working consistently to meet their own goals.

Keep your goals achievable and something that you can do on a day-to-day basis. When you do this, you will find that you are becoming consistent in your life and what you are doing becomes a routine. Then you will find yourself making more sales calls on a regular basis, instead of once in a while. This applies to new sales calls as well as visiting your past customers.

Where are you with respect to your sales month-to-date (exactly), and at what percentage of quota? (Example: 243 percent) Now, where are you year-to-date with respect to your quota? If you can answer these two questions without looking at any paperwork, you are goal oriented!

[ACTION STEP]

Take a little time to look at what goals you will have for the year. Then break them down by each quarter of the year so you can manage them more easily.

Goals for the year:

1st quarter goals:

2nd quarter goals:

3rd quarter goals:

4th quarter goals:

Quiz 10

1. A goal without a plan is

   A. Achievable.

   B. A wish.

   C. The winning point in a game.

   D. Underrated.

2. You can do work-related tasks

   A. Out of the office.

   B. Only at the office.

   C. For just an hour a day.

   D. While you sleep.

3. A good goal has a specific time frame, is measurable, is realistic, and

   A. Is challenging.

   B. Is easy.

    C. Is impossible.

    D. Has no merit.

4. To achieve your goals, it's best to

    A. Have other people work on them for you.

    B. Break them down into smaller steps or pieces.

    C. List them on a paper and forget about them.

    D. Talk about them with your friends.

Closing the Sale

"Larry, I know you're trying to close this deal, but I just don't see the need for electric dog polishers. Our company manufactures dog food."

Cartoon © Priyanka Pai. Used with permission.

LESSON 42

It's Not What You Think

When you ask for the order, which of these symptoms do you experience?

    A. Sweaty palms.

    B. Paralysis.

    C. Shaking knees.

    D. All of the above.

I ask people attending my seminars which they think is harder. Is it harder to close for an appointment? This involves calling a prospect on the phone, identifying yourself, saying you'd like to ask some questions, and then closing for an appointment. Or, is it harder to close for an order? This involves sitting in front of the customer, asking your questions, and then asking if the customer wants the product. Anywhere from 40 to 60 percent of the salespeople I talk to think it's harder to close for the sale. I truly believe they imagine closing to be harder than it actually is. Here are my reasons why.

The customer knows your job is to sell her a product or service. The customer, therefore, *expects you at some point in the process to ask for the order.* In my opinion, it's harder to ask for the appointment, because I'm asking for a portion of her time. If I'm in front of her, she expects me to ask her to buy my product. If I came to your house to talk to you about insurance, you'd be waiting for me to say, "Do you want it?" If I gave you a quote on replacing your roof, you'd be waiting for me to say, "Is this something you're interested in purchasing?"

Think about all the times you desperately want to buy something and just want to get the process done with. The first challenge you face is that you have to make dozens of decisions. I swear, the most confusing thing you can do is to go into a store to buy a pair of jeans. You have to decide whether you want a straight cut, boot cut, or some other cut. Do you want a zipper or button fly? Do you want acid wash, stone wash, or a darker look? Once you've decided all that and found a pair that actually fits, you proceed to the counter where you're faced with another decision: cash or credit card. In my opinion, every customer you deal with goes through the same process in one form or another. When you're in front of the prospect, it's your job to make the process as easy as possible for him by presenting the choices in the form of questions so he can painlessly come up with the answer. When this process is over, he will actually be anxious for you to ask the question, "Do you want it?" In other words, closing is not as difficult as you may expect it to be and is often a relief to the customer!

Lesson 43

Half the Game Is Watching

Approach closing like a game. There are as many moves and strategies as there are people. The good news is that you can learn to close successfully by doing one thing: watching your customer.

Learn how to read your customer. Does he appear interested or bored? Pay attention to his body language and how he responds to your questions. In particular, watch the customer's eyes and smile. In most cases, the eyes and smile will reveal how he feels.

Some people just want you out of their offices, so they may agree in principle to the sale just to end the conversation. After some practice, you will learn how to spot the people who are overly agreeable to everything you say. Remember, interested customers are ones who ask questions. They are engaged in the conversation.

Don't get arrogant or cute. Always be professional. If you're ever in front of a customer who becomes inappropriate by swearing a lot, do *not* behave likewise. Stay professional. All professionals do this. If you go to the dentist and say, "This *!@#$% tooth is killing me," you'll never hear your dentist say, "Yeah, I know what you mean, the same *!@#$% thing happened to the *!@#$% patient before you." Never!

The Father of Closing Techniques

The successful closing techniques of 70 years ago are still valid today. In my first book, *Can I Have Five Minutes of Your Time?*, I included the techniques of J. Douglas Edwards, who was known as the father of closing techniques. The closes might seem a little corny today, but none the less, they are still used every day by salespeople.

One example might be the "either/or" close. A good example is if you are at a McDonald's and the cashier asks if you would like a medium or large fry with your meal, putting you in a position in which you must buy. Another one might be the "puppy dog" close, in which you let someone take the product or service home for a couple of days for a free trial to see if they like it. Most people keep the "puppy" after they have had it for a few days due to their new found attachment.

Years ago, when I was first given these closes, guess what I did? I put them on the shelf. A few years later, I thought, "Maybe they've got something here." I decided to look at closing from a different angle: as a chess game. Wouldn't it be fun to always be in control, to be one step ahead in a sales conversation, to try different things with the customer and see what happens?

I decided to memorize these closes and to use different closes in different situations. I would ask myself, "Which of these closes should I use?" One day, while I was waiting in the lobby to see the decision-maker, I picked up my notepad and wrote down the close I would try that day. An amazing thing happened. Selling became much more fun, because I made it a game.

You know from other areas of your life that if you just do the same thing all the time, it gets boring. If you do different things all the time, life is more fun. Apply the same idea to closing; try different approaches and make a game out of it.

I am a *huge* fan of the trial close, the "If I... then will you...?" example. What I love about the trial close is that it gets right to the point and is very effective. Using the trial close combined with great questions will allow you to measure the level of interest of the customer. It can be the only close you have to use, if you are asking the right questions. Trial closes will be covered more extensively in the next section. Understanding closing techniques, such as the ones used by J. Douglas Edwards, will give you knowledge and make your selling day a little more fun for both you and your customer.

It's time to go out and start practicing what's in this chapter, but not on your customer. Do it in role-play situations with your family or friends. Save the customer for when you are truly ready. Pros don't play the game until they've practiced.

The Trial Close

Many companies call and ask me to help their salespeople close better in the selling process. Weak salespeople close hard. Let me repeat that: weak salespeople close hard. Closing is a skill learned by salespeople to get the order. The problem is that most salespeople close for the order before finding out what the customer wants and needs. Don't you hate it when you go into a business to buy a big-ticket item, such as a new car, copier, or furniture, and the salesperson pressures you to buy?

Many companies think these are good selling skills and that their salespeople are doing a fine job. Not even close! They are not forming relationships that will lead to return customers. The customer won't tell his family, friends, or coworkers about what a wonderful experience he had buying the product or service.

The problem is that the salesperson didn't use a trial close. A trial close sets everything up in a logical, straightforward manner that lets the customer participate in the sales process. The whole premise behind the trial close is simple: "If I..., will you...?" This will work in any sales situation and is most effective toward the beginning of the conversation.

Here's an example. "Reader, if you like my book, would you be interested in buying any of my books or bringing me in to train your salespeople?" This is right to the point and will elicit a response, because you have asked a question that requires a yes or no response. If you say yes, that's great. I just have to ask you some more questions to find out the rest of your needs. If you say no, all I have to do is say two simple words: "Why not?"

You have heard me go on and on about the use of questions in the sales process to gather information on the customer and/or company. This is what salespeople are supposed to do—period. If you don't believe me, just pick up any book on sales by a notable author and it will say the same thing: selling is asking, not telling.

Through the use of more questions, you can find out whether you have a prospect. If not, it's time to move on. If you are a prospect, then I will spend more time asking questions and maybe even schedule another visit.

Pretend we're in a car dealership, and we want to start the process of looking for a new car. The salesperson greets us and then for a minute or so asks us a few basic questions and starts to build rapport with us. Next, the salesperson says, "If I can find the car you want, I'll take four percent off the sticker price, because there is only an eight percent markup. This way you'll get a good price, we'll make a small profit, and the price will be competitive to any dealer in the country because we all pay the same price from the manufacturer." Wouldn't that put you more at ease? We got right down to it and didn't have to haggle.

The more a salesperson uses a trial close, the less he or she will use pressure closes in the selling process. If the salesperson uses a good trial close and asks a lot of high-quality questions, he or she actually won't have to do any closing. Why? It's simple. Customers will tell you what they want to buy, when they want to buy, how they want to buy, and usually how much they will pay.

Remember, a trial close and many questions are the key to a sale.

[ACTION STEP]

What are the trial closes that work well with your product or service?

1.

2.

3.

4.

5.

Quiz 11

1. Salespeople often mistakenly think that the hardest part of a sale is
   A. Making an appointment.
   B. Filling out an order form.
   C. Dressing appropriately.
   D. Closing.

2. The father of closing techniques is
   A. Michael Jordan.
   B. Bill Clinton.
   C. J. Douglas Edwards.
   D. Bill Gates.

3. A trial close is

    A. If I… will you….

    B. Why won't you buy from me?

    C. What will it take to get your business?

    D. An attorney's closing arguments.

4. A trial close is best used

    A. In the beginning of the sale.

    B. At the end of the sale.

    C. To rescue a sale.

    D. Any time during the sale.

Customer Care

"Cary, I appreciate you stopping by to say hello, but I keep telling you that these are pictures of my family and they don't need new windows."

Cartoon © Julie Selby. Used with permission.

LESSON 46

Customer Service Warranty Card

After the sale, you have to work at keeping customers happy, so they will want to do business with you again. It's important to follow up with current customers by asking questions about their satisfaction with the product or service you sold them. Knowing that you are there to handle any problems builds confidence and trust. That's all part of good customer service. (In addition to sales, customer service is one of my great passions and the topic of another one of my books, *Lip Service*.)

As soon as you finish this, go to my Website, Halbecker.com, and click "Power Tools," then download this card. It's now yours to use as you want. Put your logo on it, blow it up to the size of a football field, wallpaper your office with it— just use it! The information is basic, right to the point, and easy to implement.

The problem is that most companies talk a good game when it comes to customer service. What company says, "We really aren't that good, but our advertising would lead you to believe that we are"? It's hard to go two days and not experience poor service somewhere. Either we are expecting less or the company is giving us less. Whichever the case, it's still not right.

Customer Service Warranty Card

This card is null and void if you fail to follow and produce these terms and conditions.

To be the best, you are:

1. UNDERSTANDING—Customer service is not about what you think, but what the customer thinks.

2. CREATIVE—Customer service is *doing more* for the customer than the customer expects.

3. NICE—Realize customers may not always be right, but they are in charge.

And remember:

- Selling is asking not telling, listening not talking.
- People buy from people.

Service is an attitude with rules attached. They go hand-in-hand; without one, the other is useless and vice versa. I'm amazed at how simple good customer service is to provide when companies use a little training, follow simple procedures, and have managers who monitor what their salespeople are doing. If you think about good customer service, the world's best companies do it and the rest talk about doing it or just pretend they are doing it.

To be great at customer service, you must be:

- **Understanding.** Customer service is not what you think but what the customer thinks. Imagine having bad food or bad service at a restaurant. What do most people say? "Don't go to that restaurant. The service was terrible and the food was awful." I never hear people say, "Don't go to that restaurant, but if you have to, make sure you don't get Becky for a waitress or Bob for a cook!" Here's another example. Your waitress asks, "How was everything?" You respond, "Lousy." The server replies, "How about a free dessert?" She doesn't know that you're on day two of a strict diet and you could eat the paste off the wallpaper if it was sweet, and now you're even more upset about the terrible food you ate because it was your only meal for the day. What the server should have said was, "What would you like to make this right?" Now you have choices and are more likely to leave the restaurant happy.

- **Creative.** Customer service is *doing more* for the customer than the customer expects. Think about the last time you took your car in for service at the dealership or service station. Has your car ever been ready sooner than they promised or the bill less than they quoted it? Imagine when you picked up your car that it was washed and the inside vacuumed. Improbable, but why not? If they had done more for you than expected, the chances are likely that you would be a loyal, lifelong customer.

- **Nice.** It's important to realize that the customer may not be right, but they are in charge. You have undoubtedly heard the line "The customer is always right." The customer is rarely right, but when you say no to them you also risk saying goodbye to their business, their money, and your profit! Let the customer think they are right and you will retain their business. People like to feel important and that they won't be challenged or argued with.

Lastly, remember that people buy from people. Customers like to do business with people they like. You should leave with a good feeling when you give your money or business to someone. We frequent the places that give us good service, outstanding value, and above all, a good feeling that makes us want to come back. A good experience also means we tell others about the encounter and how satisfied we were.

Remember, great people with great attitude give great service. It's simple: the better the attitude, the better the service. One other thing: the company needs to back up their culture of providing great customer service with some good policies that empower its employees to make the decision on a one-by-one case.

Why Customer Service Is Important

Why do most companies say that they care about customer service but do very little to improve it? The hard part of business is getting the customer. The easy part is keeping them. I guarantee that if you tell this to some company's senior management, they'll disagree with me, because in their experience, they have failed to keep business due to poor customer service. Unfortunately, they have also failed to understand that this is why they are losing business.

Keeping customers, and keeping them happy, isn't difficult. A friend of mine once told me that *you should acquire customers and then convert them into clients.* All that is necessary is being honest and taking care of people the way you would like them to take care of you. In most people's sales approach, they promise customers that if they buy the product or service, after the sale the customer will be taken care of like a king.

Then what happens? Nothing, zippo, zada, zilch! Promises are broken, and people end up frustrated. Let me ask you a question: if you only had one customer, how would you treat him or her? Pretty good, I'll bet! Why can't we apply this concept to all customers? Give them what they want instead of ducking or avoiding their problems. Take care of the situation immediately without giving excuses. Now you will be able to keep your promise of taking care of customers. Chances are, you will also become a hero to them!

Imagine this scenario: You go to a restaurant and the food is good, but the waitress is terrible and has a bad attitude. She makes you feel that it's almost a favor for her to serve your food or to get you another cup of coffee. What about this? You have the same meal, but now the waitress is outstanding, sweet, bubbly, and doing more than you expect to provide you with a wonderful dining experience. Which person will receive a larger tip? In fact, which waitress do you even want to give a tip? It makes us feel good to reward someone who does a good job. As a sales trainer, I find it interesting that the same thing happens in sales. If the salesperson is doing a good job, he or she is rewarded with commission.

To truly be successful in business, you have to not only get customers, but maintain your customer base while keeping expenses such as advertising low. Customer satisfaction is the easiest way to reduce your advertising and marketing costs. It allows you to rely on plain-old word-of-mouth advertising. It is, and will always be, the best form of getting business. Good customer service *is* good business.

Here are some very interesting statistics from TARP in its study, *A National Survey of the Complaint Handling Procedures Used by Consumers* (NTIS PB-263-082 Washington, DC: White House Office of Consumer Affairs 1976):

- The average business does not hear from 96 percent of its unhappy customers.

- A customer who has a bad experience with a business will tell about 9 to 10 other people and about 13 percent will tell more than 20 people.

- For every complaint received at company headquarters, the average business has another 26 with problems and at least 6 of those are serious ones.

- About 65 to 90 percent of your non-complainers will not buy from you again and you will never know why.

- Surveys show that you can win back between 54 and 70 percent of these customers by simply resolving their complaints, the majority of whom will become loyal customers,

So what can you do to ensure great customer satisfaction?

- Solicit complaints and make it easy for unhappy customers to tell you what their problems are.

- Solve their complaints as quickly as possible and with a smile.

- Keep records of why complaints occur, analyze how complaints can be prevented, and then make any changes to your procedures to ensure customer satisfaction.

- Provide incentives to encourage your employees to want to create great customer loyalty.

If you start doing things with the customer in mind and not your sales, watch and see your marketing costs go down and customer satisfaction go up!

The Joey

Remember the TV show *Friends*? One of the best lessons you can learn in sales and customer service was derived from this sitcom. The lesson was there almost every week and few people took advantage of figuring out what it was. If you did catch on, it provided the opportunity to change your relationships not only in the world of business, but also with your family and friends.

Enough build-up; here it is: I call it "The Joey." Remember the character Joey Tribbiani, the good looking neighbor played by Matt LaBlanc? When he met a girl, which was about every episode, he always asked, with his famous smile, "How you doin'?"

This can be used instantly on any customer to find out what is going on. In a sales situation you can find out where the customer stands by just asking, "How are you doing?" Be direct and to the point. Let her know you are serious about making sure that she is a satisfied customer. Most salespeople don't ask the real question, because their focus is on the sale and not the customer.

Many times the salesperson is afraid that the answer might be negative, that the customer is unsatisfied, or there is a chance she will take her business elsewhere. The key to asking this question is being sincere. Show that you care and are interested in the answer, regardless of what the answer is. The trick is to do this with every customer all the time, not just a few or the ones you think will give you the answer you are looking for. If you avoid your dissatisfied customers, you are guaranteeing that they will not be a customer for long. I know it takes more work on your part, but think of the time you will save in not having to generate new customers to replace them. This will be especially beneficial to customers with whom you don't have a firmly established relationship yet. Follow-up phone calls after the sale should be a regular part of doing business. Remember: be proactive, rather than reactive, in your customer service. Rather than wait around to hear from your customers, make the calls to your client base and reach out to find their level of satisfaction and why they are doing business with you or your company.

Staying in touch with clients is imperative. Most salespeople don't follow up with their clients, let alone stay in touch with them over a long period of time. They don't take the time or put in the effort to build a relationship with the client or customer. Once the sale is over, the salesperson is on to the next sale. Some salespeople might write the obligatory thank-you note or some take the easy way out and send a quick e-mail. Does that really build a relationship? Does it really let someone know how much you appreciate his business and thank him for trusting you? Does it really thank the client for picking you over the competition?

[ACTION STEP]

Here are some sample customer-care questions or your "Joeys."

- Are you pleased with our service or product?
- Is there anything that you are not happy with?
- Is there anything that we can do to better serve you?

What is your "Joey"?

Lesson 49

Sucking Up

Great relationships take time and plenty of "sucking up." Now what do I mean by that? Forget all the negative connotations associated with the term. *Sucking up* should be a term used as flattery and viewed as something you do with sincerity. In this sense it means catering to the whims of the client, making totally sure they are happy, going out of your way to please them, and always being there in the future when they need something. The more you stay in touch with a customer, the more you'll learn about him, including his current and future product needs. You'll also learn what he likes and doesn't like about your company. Think how one simple, easily accomplished idea to improve one small aspect of your company could win you friends with your company's management. In the end, you get accolades from both your customer and your company, simply because you stayed in touch and asked questions.

I like being associated with clients who have a sense of humor. It's alright to have fun with people, as long as your behavior is appropriate and you do your job to the best of your abilities. Right after conducting a speech for a company or an association, I will

209

call my contact and say, "Hi, this is Hal, and I want to thank you for bringing me in. This is my suck-up call to see if you were pleased with the speech, content, etc." I have never had anyone complain or be bothered by the call or the voicemail I left if they were unavailable. It's quite the opposite. They call back and say that they laughed when they heard my message. The key is to call them as quick as you can and let them know that you care. Be sincere and don't just go through the motions.

I have mentioned before that there has never been an instance where I've asked for a referral. My business during the last 27 years as a sales consultant has been 100 percent word-of-mouth. This was simple to do by sucking up and constantly staying in touch with my clients over the years.

These constant touch points with my clients were not self-serving. Many times I would call and remind them that if they were looking for speakers for additional meetings they should contact me. I already know their audience and what they might like or dislike. Doing this also gives me an inside track to some of the other speakers who are in my industry that would be a good fit. Sucking up can happen in any way you want, as long as you make it about the client and not yourself. Think about what they might want rather than what you want to sell!

A good question is where to begin. First, think of who you are going to call and why you are making the call. Then write out what you want to say. Try leaving yourself a practice voicemail to see how you sound. Are you coming through as genuine or sounding like a phony? The more you practice, the more comfortable you will be with reaching out to your customers.

Why CRAP Is Important!

To really get the most out of life and your career, you have to go by the rules of the game. Yes, both life and work are a game. There are a set of rules, or play book, to follow and a period of time allowed to play the game. There are also consequences if you don't follow the rules. The key to the game is simple, and it's easy to be in the winner's circle most of the time once you realize that it's all CRAP! I know I said the word CRAP, and if this offends you please stop reading. Of course, you'll miss the beauty of CRAP. Once you understand how wonderful CRAP is to follow, you will be amazed at your results. Let's get into some CRAP now!

- **Caring.** You must care about what you're doing. This goes for your job, family, and friends. I want to be around an airline pilot who cares about safety, a surgeon who cares about the patient, a mother who cares about her child, or a salesperson who cares about the customer. The ability and willingness to care is a number-one priority for a meaningful and prosperous life.

- **Relationships.** The deeper your relationships, the more enriched your life will be. Do you want to go though life with surface, meaningless relationships or deep ones where you get to know and understand the other person? Do you want the type of relationship where another person is always there for you and vice versa, no matter what happens? Relationships aren't just with friends and family, but also involve coworkers, clients, or customers.

- **Attitude.** I love being around people who have a positive attitude about everything. They are always trying to be better at something, no matter what it is. It can be an attitude about their job or family, or even about the appearance of their home's front lawn. When you have attitude about something, you try to make it better and that involves thought, time, and usually hard work. Attitude describes the mood you are in and how you are going to go about the thought process at hand. Attitude determines outcome!

- **Passion.** Without passion, we're all mediocre. Passion is the difference between average and great. I love being around great people for many reasons. You can learn from them, and what a joy it is to watch someone who truly excels at what they do. Would you rather watch me or Tiger Woods play golf? Who would you rather watch play basketball, Lebron James, Michael Jordan, or Woody Allen? I take that back, I think watching Woody Allen play basketball would be rather amusing.

Put the four letters—C-R-A-P—together and see what you have each and every time. Excellence! To win at the game of life or business, you need to find the excellence inside of you that allows you to bring out the important qualities needed for success. CRAP is all of them in a nice little package.

Quiz 12

1. You should acquire customers and then convert them into
   A. Mindless idiots who do everything you say.
   B. Friends.
   C. Clients.
   D. Enemies.

2. Customer satisfaction is the easiest way to
   A. Reduce your advertising and marketing cost.
   B. Not have to visit or call customers.
   C. Sit around a campfire and sing songs.
   D. Never have to say you're sorry.

3. Most customers do not
   A. Spend money.
   B. Tell war stories.
   C. Drink coffee.
   D. Complain.

4. A customer who has an unpleasant experience with a company will tell
   A. Four people.
   B. Nine to 10 people.
   C. Everyone they know
   D. No one.

5. The character Joey is from the TV show
   A. *Buddies.*
   B. *Cheers.*
   C. *Friends.*
   D. *NYPD Blue.*

6. Joey uses the phrase
   A. "How are we doing?"
   B. "How is the family?"
   C. "How's business?"
   D. "How *you* doin'?"

7. Salespeople also need to place

   A. Friendly calls.

   B. Inquisitive calls.

   C. Follow up calls.

   D. All of the above.

Role-Playing

"Okay, when the instructor comes back from the bathroom, are we all agreed that we tell him we already finished the role-plays?"

LESSON 51

Role-Playing Exercise

Most professions practice regularly. One of the few exceptions? Salespeople. Where do most salespeople practice? On their customers *during* the sales call! One way to improve, in addition to reading sales books or taking courses, is to use role-playing. It's an excellent way to practice and improve skills that have been learned in a classroom setting.

Here are the steps to a role-play session that allows you to practice sales situation:

1. **Define the topic for the role-play.** Every role-play session should have a topic. Topics can include greeting customers, gaining rapport, asking questions, learning customer's needs, closing sales, handling objections, and so on. Topics can be chosen to fit whatever area or concept you want to improve.

2. **Choose the players.** Say there are 15 people in the room. You should divide them into groups of three people. Be mindful in your selections, attempting to group people who don't usually work together. You

don't want people role-playing with the person they're sitting next to. The idea is to interact with other people.

One person will be the salesperson, another the customer, and the third person will be the observer. The person playing the customer should be somewhat demanding by asking tough questions or by saying no to buying. The person playing the salesperson should practice asking questions rather than talking during the sales call. This practice is extremely beneficial. The observer is the most important person. She should be taking copious notes and writing what she noticed. Her notes shouldn't be limited to what was done correctly or incorrectly, but rather should try to capture the whole picture as if she were a critic reviewing a movie.

3. **Allow the salesperson to discuss his or her performance.** After completing the role-play, the next step is to give the person playing the salesperson an opportunity to tell the group what he or she could have done better.

4. **Allow the observer to discuss what he or she saw.** It's now the observer's turn to share his or her thoughts on what the salesperson did well and what needs improvement. The more thought that goes into the observing role, the more the salesperson would benefit.

Remember that this is practice, and practice is what makes people better in their careers. In these three-person role-plays, each person has the opportunity to play the position of the salesperson, customer, and observer. This way, they can all offer their thoughts and ideas. The complete process takes about 45 minutes, or 15 minutes for each role-play.

There is no such thing as one way to do things. Role-playing allows salespeople to get more comfortable in their selling process. The practice sessions give them the tools and confidence necessary to improve their own selling skills.

It is not easy for a sales person to role-play. Sometimes it might feel too "staged" or unrealistic. It's important to relax, make it as real as possible, and get into the action. Role-playing shouldn't be an occasional thing. You need to continually practice the same way a football or basketball team practices to maintain their skills and improve.

The Roles in a Role-Playing Exercise

Each role in the exercise plays a significant and specific part.

Let's say you are the salesperson, and you have just made a first appointment with a prospect. Your goal is to find out about her company and needs. Ask questions that pertain to:

- Operations.

- Decision-making.

- Use of product or service.

- Current vendor or company she uses.

- Dissatisfaction (if any).

In this case, you're the buyer, and this is your first meeting with the salesperson. Everything you have heard sounds good, but you'd like a little more time to think about it. Be a little tough, but not too rough on the salesperson. Don't be a pushover, just a real buyer who has a few real objections before you buy. When you are asked to buy, you say, "I would like some time to think about it."

If you are the observer, your role is to watch and listen to what the salesperson says and how the prospect reacts. Here are some things to look for:

- Did the seller ask good questions to find out about the company and their needs?

- Was the salesperson with the right decision-maker?

- Were there some buying signals from the buyer that went unnoticed?

- Were any objections handled adequately?

- Was the buyer's resistance real or contrived?

- Did the seller seem genuine?

- Did the seller actually close for the sale or a second appointment?

- Did the seller talk too much?

If you are the sales manager running the exercise, follow the instructions on this form.

◆◆◆

Salesperson:

Date:

Customer Observed:

Sit there and BE QUIET. Your role as the manager is to watch, listen and provide IMPORTANT feedback so the sales rep will know how they performed on the call.

It's now time to take detailed notes of the sales call.

PRE-CALL: Is the sales rep prepared? Does he/she have his/her questionnaire and does he/she have all the information and "tools" necessary for the call?

SALES CALL: Be specific and provide pros and cons. Look for what he did right, wrong, and anything she could have done.

Strengths and Areas for Improvement

Ability to build rapport:

Qualifying and questioning skills:

Listening skills:

Presentation:

Handling objections:

Gaining commitment:

Trial close and other closes:

◆◆◆

Quiz 13

1. Role-playing allows salespeople to

    A. Share their feelings.

    B. Become friends with their managers.

    C. Practice.

    D. Earn commission.

2. In role-play, it's best to group people who

    A. Usually don't work together.

    B. Are best friends.

    C. Are new to the company.

    D. Are sales veterans.

3. After role-playing, the salesperson should discuss his or her

    A. Life.

    B. Performance.

C. Favorite movies.

D. Most embarrassing moment.

4. In role-playing exercises, the observer must

A. Describe what he or she saw.

B. Mock the participants.

C. Ignore the exercise.

D. Praise only his or her friends.

You've Earned a Bonus!

"John, you have a great smile and I know you're trying to interview well, but you're freaking me out."

Using PowerPoint Like a Pro

In today's high-tech business environment, you see PowerPoint or Keynote presentations everywhere. Used heavily in business meetings, they can be seen in boardrooms all across the world. These presentations are used in situations that involve someone trying to get his or her message or idea across to others. I get a kick out of how bad some of these presentations are and how the participants are subjected to watching a poor performance. I have never heard anyone say, "Hey, my PowerPoint sucks. I wish I could take a class or learn how to do it right from someone who really knows this stuff!" Read on, and you will know what it takes to capture an audience by the end of this lesson.

Think about your favorite comedian, minister, or rabbi. Have you ever seen any of them use PowerPoint in delivering their message? I doubt it. Their mission is to capture the audience and get their point across while the audience is focused on them. They know that if they use a projector and screen, it will take the emphasis off of them and focus it elsewhere. It's an unhealthy dynamic for an audience when there is confusion about where to look. The presenter wants the audience to respond to him or her and not be distracted.

The master of Keynote was Apple's former CEO Steve Jobs. He was the best! If you don't believe me and you want to see the master in action, go to YouTube and type in "Steve Jobs iPod." Here you will see him introduce a wildly popular product to the world by use of a computerized presentation program. To truly understand this example, you should watch his presentation.

Steve Jobs was a genuine showman. He knew what his audience wanted, and he delivered it with his own style. He was comfortable on stage and passionate about what he was presenting. He was also having fun. All of this equates into a captive audience.

Most people make their PowerPoint presentation the same as their handout. Bad move! People don't need you to read the presentation off the screen. They can do that themselves! Longer is not better. As a presenter, your PowerPoint presentation should have a minimum number of slides and each slide should contain only a few key concepts. Steve Jobs displayed only a few words on his Keynote slide *after* he told you something. What this did was reinforce his idea while keeping the focus on him. He employed the perfectly balanced technique of presenting and reinforcing his concepts. His remarkable and comfortable style was not about heavy text or statistics. It was designed to engage you and get you excited about what he was discussing.

Steve Jobs was a storyteller. To keep you interested, he did not give away the whole plot right away. He disclosed things slowly and built up to the big reveal. Basically, what he was doing was taking you along on a journey, building momentum as he presented.

You don't have to be an incredible showman like Steve Jobs was to accomplish this yourself. Just remember that less is more, and the presentation should not duplicate your handout. It's a tool to get people excited about the message you're delivering.

One more thing: Steve Jobs made it look effortless because he rehearsed. Do you?

Selling the Interview

As a sales consultant who works with organizations to help them improve their sales process, what still surprises me is that most people don't have a clue on how to interview properly. The interview is a simple, common-sense process. Whether you are selling a product, a service, or even yourself, it's still sales. Call it what you want, but the object is to get the other person to buy into what you are selling. In an interview, the product is you, and the service is what you are going to do for your employer after you are hired.

Regardless of which company or industry I work with, or the experience level of the salesperson—from newly hired to seasoned veteran—the same issue always is brought up. I have to *force* most salespeople to write out what questions they want to ask the client or prospect. Time and time again, the salesperson wants to go in and "wing it" with no preparation, just what is in his head. He is fine with going on a sales call and just "seeing what will happen." As far as I am concerned, that's just plain stupid!

Let's go through a couple of key things that you need to do during the interview if you have any interest in getting hired.

- **Ask prepared questions.** This is where you're going to spend most of your preparation time. The more *they* talk and the less *you* talk about yourself, the better your chances. Yes, you heard me right. Let them talk! People love to hire a good listener, and nobody likes to be around anyone who constantly talks about themselves. Go in prepared with at least 10 to 15 written questions. It's okay to pull out these questions during the interview. The person interviewing you will be impressed that you took the time to prepare for the interview.

    Here are some great questions to use during the interview.

    ‣ Why is this position currently open? If it is not a new position, what happened to the previous person?

    ‣ What could I do differently than the person who had the position prior to me?

    ‣ What is most pressing? What would you like to have accomplished in the short and long term?

    ‣ What are the traits needed for someone to excel in this position?

    ‣ Can you describe a typical day in this position?

    ‣ I am very interested in the job, what is the next step?

    These are just a few samples. Each job interview needs to have specific questions that will align with the job and the person or department involved.

- **Notice things.** Look around the room or office you are in during or before the interview. Does it seem like a relaxed place to work or does the design theme remind you of a prison? As you are walking to the office where the interview is going to be held, do other employees seem happy and are they enjoying themselves, or is the place run like a sweat shop?

- **Ask for a tour.** This is where you can get a great feel for the company. Do they take pride in what they do? Is management fully engaged? Is the CEO accessible or in an ivory tower? Does it seem like a place where you can advance as you further your career?

- **Wear middle-of-the-road clothing.** Don't stand out to the point that your clothing gets you noticed. Your personality should do this for you. Men and women should be dressed in a professional manner and always have immaculate grooming. The way you are dressed should not define who you are and should be appropriate for the job for which you are applying.

Always remember the linchpin to the interviewing process is to make it past the first interview. You will need multiple interviews before you are hired. Finally, make sure you don't limit yourself to one company.

Cancer and the
Importance of Questions

This is very personal, but I feel that sharing it is necessary. This happened to me in December 1982. On Christmas Eve, I felt a pain in my stomach. Because I work out quite a bit, I thought I had pulled a muscle, so I backed off from my sit-ups for a few weeks. Well, a couple months later, the pain was still there.

Being the brave guy that I am, I finally mustered enough courage to go to the doctor to check out the situation. First, he wanted to do an ultrasound. I knew this was a painless procedure, so I said, "Fine." Next, he wanted to do a CAT scan. I asked if this procedure involved any needles. Again, I said, "Fine, let's do it." The results were devastating. When he called me into an exam room and said he wanted to speak with me, I still thought he was going to tell me I had pulled some muscles and that he would give me some Bengay and send me on my way. Instead, he laid a bombshell on me and explained that I had terminal cancer. The lymph nodes throughout my abdomen were enlarged and were positive for cancer. This, of course, was not what I wanted to hear.

The doctor explained that the course of treatment was eight to nine hours of intensive surgery to remove the lymph nodes, followed by eight months of chemotherapy. I didn't want to hear this, especially with all the undesirable side effects. He also said that if I did nothing, I had five to six months to live. Surgery and chemotherapy would improve my odds to 30 percent or so. I said I needed a little time to think about this dilemma. Here's where it's important to do your homework and learn as much as possible about the subject presented to you. I found out that in cancer research, someone does a study, called a protocol, and if it's successful, then other doctors around the United States follow that protocol in their own hospital. In my personal search, I discovered that the author of the paper on my cancer was Dr. Larry Einhorn at the University of Indiana.

I made an appointment to see him and took my test results to get his opinion on what to do. His words were simple, cold, and right to the point, "If you don't do the surgery, you'll die. End of story. Those are your options, your only options." I didn't want to hear that. I was trying to avoid the surgery for a number of reasons. I came back home and went to Dr. Martin Resnick, the head of urology at the largest teaching hospital in Cleveland, University Hospitals. I asked him about the surgery, and he said it was a serious surgery, and it was the recommended procedure. I then asked a few questions. This was my life we were talking about, and I had done my homework! I asked, "What will cure my cancer, the surgery or the chemotherapy?" He explained that the surgery was necessary to stage the cancer, but that the chemotherapy, if successful, was what would ultimately cure me. I then said, "Tell me more about the chemotherapy, and why this will cure me and not the surgery."

After listening to his explanation I asked the second most important question of my life (the most important question being to ask my wife if she would marry me): "Why not skip the surgery and just do the chemo, and we can see if the tumors shrink or dissipate by continuing to do ongoing CAT scans, and then compare the results to the present CAT scan?"

To my amazement, he said this idea wasn't the standard protocol, but it had some merit. He said that it was very risky, and that I was gambling with my life. I explained that it is my life, and the side effects of the surgery were too great and would not give me the quality of life I desired, especially as I was 28 years old at that time. That conversation happened 30 years ago, and it was a successful gamble. The bottom line is that I went into a negotiation with my doctor. With a little knowledge based on some investigative work and lots of questions, I was able to make a very serious decision. The result could have gone either way: it could have been devastating, or it could have provided me with a quality and fulfilling life.

This story proved to me in more ways than you can imagine the importance of questions in all aspects of life. The more you know about yourself and the other party involved, the more this information will end up being an asset to you. Remember, knowledge is power. It may even be life or death!

How Direct Opinions Got Started

A reporter called me from CBS who wanted some background stories or ideas of companies that went beyond the normal customer service experience that we are used to. She then said, "Hal, don't give me the usual Zappos, Nordstrom, Ritz Carlton examples. I would like something that is newer or fresher."

Here's the problem: I really couldn't come up with anything that stood out. Can you? What happened? Have we become so accustomed to average or poor customer service that we accept it and say, "Oh well! That is the way it is." This is bothersome to me on so many different levels that it reminds me of why I started a highly specialized customer service satisfaction firm in the early 1980s.

Let me back up a little to the mid-1970s. During that time, I had three cars stolen, all General Motors Oldsmobiles. (There were very few imports such as Honda or Toyota sold in those days.) I was getting fed up with going to get to my car, and it just wasn't there. So I decided to buy a car that would not be stolen. In those days Honda was selling a fraction of the cars that they sell today; in fact, Japanese quality was thought of as inferior to American-built cars at that time.

I bought a small Honda Prelude. My main reason was that it was cute, and no one would want to steal it. It turned out I was correct! After I bought the car, something happened that was life-changing, and it set a new course for my next occupation. After my first service on the vehicle, probably an oil change, the dealership called me to see if I was satisfied with the service performed and if the people were accommodating. Wow! I was blown away! Someone actually called me to see if I was happy, and that was radical and definitely unique in those days.

I called the dealership and asked to speak to the owner. I wanted to thank the dealership for showing its customers that they truly cared. The owner explained to me how they had a friend making the calls for them to check on the satisfaction level of the new and used car customers. I felt as though I had been hit over the head with a sledge hammer. I had always wanted my own business, but I didn't know what it would be. I was motivated to start something that was my own, and I had a few simple rules: it would involve little start-up cash (under $20,000), I did not want to manufacture anything, and all my eggs would be in small baskets. In other words, I didn't want one customer, but wanted to spread the business among many smaller customers so I didn't go out of business if I lost that "big one."

This concept fit all my rules, and I figured that there were 92 major cities in the United States so I could eventually open 92 offices, build the company up, and then sell it within 10 years, so I could retire before I was 40 years old. The concept was simple and sound: call the companies' customers and ask them three to five questions to determine their level of satisfaction and then report the results to the client.

The business plan worked, and my company Direct Opinions started to grow at a perfect pace. Before I knew it, I had half a dozen offices throughout the United States and Canada. It was hard work, because in those days auto manufacturers were not doing this type of phone survey yet, and I literally had to get one new car dealer at a time. Along with the dealership network, I also focused on making calls for large independent retailers and other industries.

To assist my office and support staff, a wonderful thing happened in 1983. IBM had just introduced their first personal computer, the XT, and I saw how this new technology could run my business and save me an immense amount of time when it came to the paperwork, bookkeeping, reports, and a sophisticated database.

In 1990, I was approached by two investors who wanted to buy me out, build the company up in other markets, and then sell the "newer and larger" company to a venture capitalist firm. They eventually fulfilled their dream as well. Today, customer follow-up is a much larger industry than just a couple start-up firms like mine in the early 1980s. It is, in many cases, the yardstick for performance standards used in industries such as hospitals, retailers, and automotive. I feel like we started a new industry and we were there in the beginning before it became truly big business.

Back to the CBS reporter and the article: I still can't think of a company for them to do a story about. Sorry!

Quiz 14

1. PowerPoint and Keynote are

    A. Board games.

    B. Cereal brands.

    C. Computerized presentation programs.

    D. Hairspray brands.

2. For a great PowerPoint presentation, you should

    A. Use many bullet points.

    B. Use as many words as possible per slide.

    C. Pack as much information in as possible.

    D. None of the above.

3. Steve Jobs was a great

    A. Comedian.

    B. Storyteller.

    C. Baseball player.

    D. CEO of Microsoft.

4. Before going on a job interview, you should

   A. Buy an expensive suit.

   B. Tell your friends that you already got the job.

   C. Write out the questions you wan to ask.

   D. Not sleep the night before.

5. On an interview, you should wear

   A. Middle-of-the-road clothing.

   B. A swimsuit.

   C. Pearls.

   D. A wool coat.

6. While on the interview, you should notice things and ask for a tour in order to

   A. Plan an escape route.

   B. Write about the company in a local paper.

   C. Make the interview feel uncomfortable.

   D. Get a better idea of the company you may be working for.

Quiz Answers

Quiz 1
1. C
2. A
3. B

Quiz 2
1. D
2. D
3. C
4. D

Quiz 3
1. D
2. B
3. A

Quiz 4
1. C
2. C
3. D
4. B
5. A
6. A
7. D

Quiz 5
1. A
2. C
3. D
4. A
5. D
6. B
7. C

Quiz 6

1. B
2. A
3. B
4. D
5. B
6. D
7. C
8. D
9. A
10. B

Quiz 7

1. A
2. C
3. D
4. B
5. C
6. A
7. D
8. D
9. B
10. D
11. B

Quiz 8

1. A
2. D
3. D
4. B

Quiz 9

1. B
2. C
3. B
4. C
5. D

Quiz 10

1. B
2. A
3. A
4. B

Quiz 11

1. D
2. C
3. A
4. D

Quiz 12

1. C
2. A
3. D
4. B
5. C
6. D
7. C

Quiz 13

1. C
2. A
3. B
4. A

Quiz 14

1. C
2. D
3. B
4. C
5. A
6. D

Index

Q

R

S

About the Author

Hal Becker is a nationally known expert on sales, customer service, and negotiating. He conducts seminars for and consults more than 140 organizations a year. His client list includes IBM, Disney, New York Life, United Airlines, Verizon, Terminix, AT&T, Pearle Vision, Cintas, and hundreds of other companies and associations.

At the age of 22, Hal became the number-one salesperson among a national sales force of 11,000 for the Xerox Corporation. Six years later, in 1983, he survived terminal cancer only months after launching Direct Opinions, one of America's first customer service telemarketing firms that facilitates more than two million calls per year with offices throughout the United States and Canada. In 1990, Hal sold Direct Opinions to devote time to consulting and presenting lectures around the world.

Hal is the author of *Can I have 5 Minutes Of Your Time?* which is now in its 21st printing and is used by many corporations as their sales bible. He has also authored two other best sellers, *Lip Service,* one of the nation's foremost books on customer service, and *Get What You Want,* a fun, upbeat, and fresh approach to negotiating.

Hal has been featured in publications including *The Wall Street Journal, Business Week, Inc. Magazine, Nations Business,* and hundreds of newspapers, radio and TV stations around the world, and is currently syndicated in over 45 newspapers and magazines.

Hal has received the Toastmasters International Communication and Leadership Award. He is one of only eight people in the world to be given this honor.

In 2010, Salesgurus.net voted Hal as one of the "World's Top 30 Professional Sales Trainers."

Inc. Magazine has voted Hal as one of the nation's top speakers in the area of sales and customer service. He is also a CSP, or Certified Speaking Professional, which is the highest earned designation presented by the National Speakers Association. The CSP award has been given less than 500 times in the past 25 years.

Hal's civic involvement is quite diverse. He is a past chairman of his local chamber of commerce and has served as a trustee of the following organizations: The Better Business Bureau, March of Dimes, Council of Smaller Enterprises, University of Akron Business School, Cleveland Health Museum/Natural History Museum, Healthy Cities Ohio, and Montefiore Nursing Home.

After battling terminal cancer, Hal founded the Cancer Hotline, a non-profit organization that provides support and assists cancer patients and their families. He donates proceeds of his books to this cause.

About Nancy Traum

Nancy Traum has devoted her career to not-for-profit organizations. From government to university positions, she is recognized as an organizational specialist. Nancy currently serves as the president/CEO of the Solon Chamber of Commerce. Her sales experience includes selling the many products and services offered by the Solon Chamber and other organizations for which she has worked. She is grateful to Hal Becker for increasing her understanding of the sales process through their working relationship.

Nancy is a strong believer in continuing education and holds a bachelors degree in communication and a masters degree in psychology with a specialty in diversity management. She is a certified diversity professional with a passion for anything involving group dynamics and corporate culture.

◆◆◆

To learn more about the seminars taught by Hal Becker, go to *www.halbecker.com*.